6 Full-Length DAT Math Practice Tests

Extra Test Prep to Help Ace the DAT Math Test

By

Michael Smith & Reza Nazari

6 Full-Length DAT Math Practice Tests

Published in the United State of America By

The Math Notion

Web: WWW.MathNotion.Com

Email: info@Mathnotion.com

About the Author

Michael Smith has been a math instructor for over a decade now. He holds a master's degree in Management. Since 2006, Michael has devoted his time to both teaching and developing exceptional math learning materials. As a Math instructor and test prep expert, Michael has worked with thousands of students. He has used the feedback of his students to develop a unique study program that can be used by students to drastically improve their math score fast and effectively.

- **SAT Math Practice Book**
- **ACT Math Practice Book**
- **GRE Math Practice Book**
- **Accuplacer Math Practice Book**
- **Common Core Math Practice Book**
- **many Math Education Workbooks, Exercise Books and Study Guides**

As an experienced Math teacher, Mr. Smith employs a variety of formats to help students achieve their goals: He tutors online and in person, he teaches students in large groups, and he provides training materials and textbooks through his website and through Amazon.

You can contact Michael via email at:

info@Mathnotion.com

Prepare for the DAT Math test with a perfect practice book!

The surest way to practice your DAT Math test-taking skills is with simulated exams. This comprehensive practice book with 6 full length and realistic DAT Math practice tests help you measure your exam readiness, find your weak areas, and succeed on the DAT Math test. The detailed answers and explanations for each DAT Math question help you master every aspect of the DAT Math.

6 Full-length DAT Math Practice Tests is a prestigious resource to help you succeed on the DAT Math test. This perfect practice book features:

- Content 100% aligned with the DAT test
- Six full-length DAT Math practice tests like the actual test in length, format, question types, and degree of difficulty
- Detailed answers and explanations for the DAT Math practice questions
- Written by DAT Math top instructors and experts

After completing this hands-on exercise book, you will gain confidence, strong foundation, and adequate practice to succeed on the DAT Math test.

WWW.MathNotion.COM

… So Much More Online!

✓ FREE Math Lessons

✓ More Math Learning Books!

✓ Mathematics Worksheets

✓ Online Math Tutors

For a PDF Version of This Book

Please Visit WWW.MathNotion.com

Contents

DAT Math Test Review

The Dental Admission Test (also known as the DAT) is a standardized test designed by the American Dental Association (ADA) to measure the general academic skills and perceptual ability of dental school applicants.

The DAT is comprised of multiple-choice test items consisting of four sections:

- ✓ Survey of the Natural Sciences
- ✓ Perceptual Ability
- ✓ Reading Comprehension
- ✓ Quantitative Reasoning

The Quantitative Reasoning section of the DAT measures applicants' math skills that will be required in dental schools. There are 40 multiple-choice questions test takers have 45 minutes to complete this section. A basic four function calculator on the computer screen will be available on this section.

In this book, we have reviewed Quantitative Reasoning topics being tested on the DAT. In this section, there are two complete DAT Quantitative Reasoning Tests. Take these tests to see what score you will be able to receive on a real DAT test.

The hardest arithmetic to master is that which enables us to count our blessings.
-Eric Hoffer

Time to Test

Time to refine your skill with a practice examination

Take a practice DAT Math Test to simulate the test day experience. After you've finished, score your test using the answer key.

Before You Start

- You'll need a pencil, a calculator and a timer to take the test.

- For each question, there are five possible answers. Choose which one is best.

- It's okay to guess. There is no penalty for wrong answers.

- Use the answer sheet provided to record your answers.

- After you've finished the test, review the answer key to see where you went wrong.

Good Luck!

DAT Practice Test 1

Quantitative Reasoning

❖ **40 Questions.**

❖ **Total time for this test: 45 Minutes**.

❖ **You may use a basic calculator on this test.**

Administered *Month Year*

1) 124 is equal to?

   A. $20 - (4 \times 10) + (6 \times 30)$

   B. $\left(\frac{11}{8} \times 72\right) + \left(\frac{125}{5}\right)$ *23.375* +

   C. $\left(\left(\frac{30}{4} + \frac{13}{2}\right) \times 7\right) - \frac{11}{2} + \frac{110}{4}$ *98*

   D. $(2 \times 10) + (50 \times 1.5) + 15$

   E. $\frac{481}{6} + \frac{121}{3}$

2) If $|a| < 2$ then which of the following is true? ($b > 0$)?

   I. $-2b < ba < 2b$ *-1 > 1*

   II. $-a < a^2 < a$ if $a < 0$ *-2 < 1*

   III. $-7 < 2a - 3 < 1$

   A. I only   C. I and III only   E. I, II and III

   B. II only   D. III only

3) Six years ago, Amy was two times as old as Mike was. If Mike is 14 years old now, how old is Amy?   *2(14−6)= Amy 16+6*

   A. 34   C. 14   E. 22

   B. 28   D. 20

4) What is the area of a square whose diagonal is 6 cm?

   A. 16 cm^2 C. 36 cm^2 E. 216 cm^2

   B. 18 cm^2 D. 33 cm^2

$a^2 + b^2 = c^2$

5) A number is chosen at random from 1 to 15. Find the probability of not selecting a composite number.

1 3 5 7 $\frac{4}{15}$

A. $\frac{1}{15}$ C. $\frac{7}{15}$ E. 0

B. 15   D. 5

6) Removing which of the following numbers will change the average of the numbers to 8?

$\frac{41-x}{5} = 8$ 40

$$1, 4, 5, 8, 11, 12$$

A. 1   C. 5   E. 12

B. 4   D. 11

7) A rope weighs 700 grams per meter of length. What is the weight in kilograms of 13.2 meters of this rope? (1 kilograms = 1000 grams)

$1 kg$ $700g \times \frac{13.2m}{1m} \times \frac{1kg}{1000g}$

A. 0.0924   C. 9.24   E. 92,400

B. 0.924   D. 9,240

8) If $y = 5ab + 2b^3$, what is y when $a = 3$ and $b = 1$?

$5(3)(1) + 2$

A. 22   C. 24   E. 17

B. 26   D. 12

9) The marked price of a computer is D dollar. Its price decreased by 40% in January and later increased by 10 % in February. What is the final price of the computer in D dollar?

A. 0.60 D   C. 0.70 D   E. 1.80 D

B. 0.66 D   D. 1.60 D

.66

1.00 D
6a ,600
.66

10) The number 60.5 is 1,000 times greater than which of the following numbers?

A. 0.605   C. 0.0650   E. 0.000605

B. 0.0605   D. 0.00605

$32 + 4x = 44 + x$
$4x = 12 + x$
$3x = 12$

11) David's current age is 44 years, and Ava's current age is 8 years. In how many years David's age will be 4 times Ava's age?

$\frac{44 + x}{8 + x} = 4$

A. 4   C. 8   E. 14

$\frac{11 + x}{2 + x} = 4$

B. 6   D. 10

$8 + 4x = x + 11$
$8 + 5x = 11$

12) How many tiles of 8 cm² is needed to cover a floor of dimension 7 cm by 32 cm?

7×32

A. 15   C. 20   E. 32

B. 18   D. 28

13) What is the value of x in the following figure?

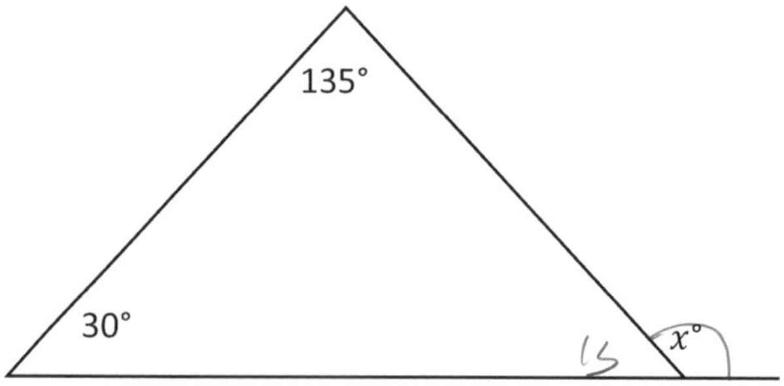

A. 150

B. 165

C. 135

D. 95

E. 105

135°

30°

$x°$

$135°$

165

14) Right triangle ABC is shown below. Which of the following is true for all possible values of angle A and B?

A. $\tan A = \tan B$

B. $\tan^2 A = \tan^2 B$

C. $\tan A = 1$

D. $\sin A = \cos B$

E. $\cot A = \sin B$

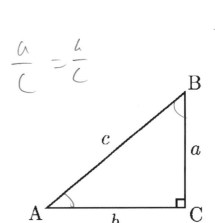

$\frac{a}{c} = \frac{b}{c}$

$\frac{b}{a} = \frac{a}{b}$

15) What is the value of y in the following system of equation?

$$4x - 2y = -20$$

$$-x + y = 10$$

$-x + \cancel{5} + 2x = 10$
$x = 5$

$2x - y = -5$
$y = 5 + 2x$

A. -4

C. 4

E. 10

B. -2

D. 5

$-x + 10 + 2x = 10$ $4x - 2y = -20$

$2x - y = -10$
$-y = -10 - 2x$
$y = 10 + 2x$

16) From the figure, which of the following must be true? (figure not drawn to scale)

A. $y = z$

B. $y = 4x$

C. $y \geq x$

D. $y + 3x = z$

E. $y > x$

$4x > x$

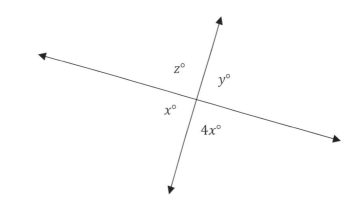

17) When 30% of 80 is added to 18% of 800, the resulting number is:

A. 36

B. 95

C. 168

D. 120

E. 175

18) A ladder leans against a wall forming a 60° angle between the ground and the ladder. If the bottom of the ladder is 40 feet away from the wall, how long is the ladder?

A. 40 feet

B. 60 feet

C. 50 feet

D. 80 feet

E. 160 feet

19) If 60 % of a class are girls, and 15 % of girls play tennis, what percent of the class play tennis?

A. 9 %

B. 12%

C. 15 %

D. 30 %

E. 60 %

20) If x is a real number, and if $x^3 + 18 = 140$, then x lies between which two consecutive integers?

A. 1 and 2

B. 2 and 3

C. 3 and 4

D. 4 and 5

E. 5 and 6

21) If $(x - 2)^3 = 8$ which of the following could be the value of $(x - 3)(x - 2)$?

A. 1

B. 2

C. 6

D. −1

E. −2

22) In five successive hours, a car travels 40 km, 42 km, 55 km, 38 km and 50 km. In the next five hours, it travels with an average speed of 60 km per hour. Find the total distance the car traveled in 10 hours.

    A. 525 km   C. 468 km   E. 1,000 km

    B. 430 km   D. 510 km

23) From last year, the price of gasoline has increased from \$1.15 per gallon to \$1.38 per gallon. The new price is what percent of the original price?

    A. 72 %   C. 140 %   E. 180 %

    B. 120 %   D. 160 %

24) If $\tan \theta = \frac{3}{4}$ and $\sin \theta > 0$, then $\cos \theta = ?$

    A. $-\frac{4}{5}$ C. $\frac{5}{12}$ E. 0

    B. $\frac{4}{5}$ D. $-\frac{12}{5}$

25) Which of the following shows the numbers in increasing order?

    A. $\frac{1}{3}, \frac{7}{11}, \frac{4}{7}, \frac{3}{4}$ D. $\frac{7}{11}, \frac{3}{4}, \frac{4}{7}, \frac{1}{3}$

    B. $\frac{1}{3}, \frac{4}{7}, \frac{7}{11}, \frac{3}{4}$ E. None of them above

    C. $\frac{4}{7}, \frac{3}{4}, \frac{7}{11}, \frac{1}{3}$

26) x is $y\%$ of what number?

    A. $\frac{x}{100y}$ C. $\frac{100x}{y}$ E. $\frac{xy}{100}$

    B. $\frac{y}{100x}$

                           D. $\frac{100y}{x}$

27) If cotangent of an angel β is 1, then the tangent of angle β is

  A. −1

  B. 1

  C. 0

  D. $\frac{1}{2}$

  E. $-\frac{1}{2}$

28) If a box contains red and blue balls in ratio of 3: 4, how many red balls are there if 80 blue balls are in the box?

  A. 90

  B. 60

  C. 30

  D. 10

  E. 8

29) 4 liters of water are poured into an aquarium that's 20cm long, 5cm wide, and 50cm high. How many cm will the water level in the aquarium rise due to this added water? (1 liter of water = 1,000 cm³)

  A. 80

  B. 40

  C. 50

  D. 10

  E. 4

30) What is the surface area of the cylinder below?

  A. $36 \pi \ in^2$

  B. $36 \pi^2 in^2$

  C. $88 \pi \ in^2$

  D. $88 \pi^2 in^2$

  E. $56 \pi \ in^2$

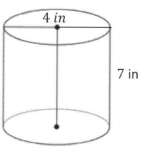

4 in

7 in

31) A chemical solution contains 3% alcohol. If there is 21ml of alcohol, what is the volume of the solution?

A. 320 ml

B. 350 ml

C. 700 ml

D. 1,200 ml

E. 1,400 ml

32) What is the solution of the following inequality?

$$|x - 8| \leq 2$$

A. $x \geq 10 \cup x \leq 6$

B. $6 \leq x \leq 10$

C. $x \geq 10$

D. $x \leq 6$

E. Set of real numbers

33) Which of the following points lies on the line $4x - y = -3$?

A. $(3, -1)$

B. $(-1, 3)$

C. $(-1, -1)$

D. $(3, -3)$

E. $(0, -3)$

34) In the following figure, ABCD is a rectangle, and E and F are points on AD and DC, respectively. The area of ΔBED is 10, and the area of ΔBDF is 12. What is the perimeter of the rectangle?

A. 20

B. 22

C. 32

D. 40

E. 44

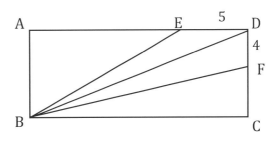

35) In the xy-plane, the point (5,6) and (4,5) are online A. Which of the following equations of lines is parallel to line A?

A. $y = 3x$

B. $y = 10$

C. $y = \frac{x}{2}$

D. $y = 2x$

E. $y = x$

36) If $f(x) = 2^x$ and $g(x) = log_2 x$, which of the following expressions is equal to $f(2g(p))$?

A. $2P$

B. 2^p

C. p^2

D. p^4

E. $\frac{p}{2}$

37) If a tree casts a 48–foot shadow at the same time that a 5 feet yardstick casts a 3–foot shadow, what is the height of the tree?

A. 14 ft

B. 30 ft

C. 80ft

D. 48 ft

E. 52 ft

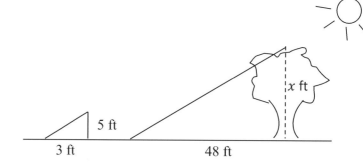

38) If the area of trapezoid is 96, what is the perimeter of the trapezoid?

A. 37

B. 42

C. 53

D. 57

E. 63

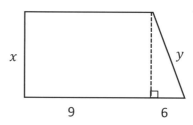

39) In the following equation when z is divided by 5, what is the effect on x?

$$x = \frac{8y + \frac{r}{r+1}}{\frac{10}{z}}$$

A. x is divided by 3

B. x is divided by 5

C. x does not change

D. x is multiplied by 5

E. x is multiplied by 3

40) If 60% of x equal to 20% of 30, then what is the value of $(x + 2)^2$?

A. 12.20

B. 24

C. 25.01

D. 1810

E. 144

STOP

This is the End of this Test. You may check your work on this Test if you still have time.

DAT Practice Test 2

Quantitative Reasoning

❖ **40 Questions.**

❖ **Total time for this test: 45 Minutes**.

❖ **You may use a basic calculator on this test.**

Administered *Month Year*

1) Convert 840,000 to scientific notation.

   A. 8.40×1000

   B. 8.40×10^{-5}

   C. 8.4×100

   D. 8.4×10^5

   E. 8.4×10^4

2) $(x^6)^{\frac{5}{8}}$ equal to?

   A. $x^{\frac{15}{4}}$

   B. $x^{\frac{53}{8}}$

   C. $x^{\frac{4}{15}}$

   D. $x^{\frac{8}{53}}$

   E. $x^{\frac{5}{48}}$

3) The average weight of 20 girls in a class is 60 kg and the average weight of 30 boys in the same class is 65 kg. What is the average weight of all the 50 students in that class?

   A. 60

   B. 63

   C. 61.28

   D. 62.90

   E. 62.48

4) If $y = (-2x^3)^2$, which of the following expressions is equal to y?

   A. $-3x^5$

   B. $-3x^6$

   C. $3x^5$

   D. $4x^5$

   E. $4x^6$

5) Sophia purchased a sofa for $399.75 The sofa is regularly priced at $615. What was the percent discount Sophia received on the sofa?

   A. 15%

   B. 35%

   C. 20%

   D. 25%

   E. 40%

6) What is the value of the expression $3(x - y) + (1 - x)^2$ when $x = 3$ and $= -4$?

    A. -8 C. 25   E. 76

    B. 18   D. 48

7) If $f(x) = 2x - 1$ and $g(x) = x^2 - 2x$, then find $\left(\frac{f}{g}\right)(x)$.

    A. $\dfrac{2x-1}{x^2-2x}$ C. $\dfrac{x-1}{x^2-1}$ E. $\dfrac{x^2-2x}{2x-1}$

    B. $\dfrac{x-1}{x^2-2x}$ D. $\dfrac{2x+1}{x^2+2x}$

8) In the standard (x, y) coordinate plane, which of the following lines contains the points $(3, -5)$ and $(8, 10)$?

    A. $y = 3x - 14$ D. $y = -\frac{1}{3}x + 14$

    B. $y = \frac{1}{3}x + 14$ E. $y = 2x - 11$

    C. $y = -3x + 7$

9) A bank is offering 2.5% simple interest on a savings account. If you deposit $15,000, how much interest will you earn in two years?

    A. \$450   C. \$4,500   E. \$4,600

    B. \$750   D. \$6,400

10) If the interior angles of a quadrilateral are in the ratio 1:2:4:5, what is the measure of the largest angle?

    A. 30°   C. 108°   E. 150°

    B. 60°   D. 120°

11) If $x + sin^2 a + cos^2 a = 3$, then $x = ?$

    A. 1   C. 3   E. 5

    B. 2   D. 4

12) If the area of a circle is 81 square meters, what is its diameter?

    A. 9π C. $\dfrac{9\sqrt{\pi}}{\pi}$ E. $9\sqrt{\pi}$

    B. $\dfrac{9}{\pi}$ D. $81\pi^2$

13) The length of a rectangle is $\dfrac{3}{4}$ times its width. If the width is 24, what is the perimeter of this rectangle?

    A. 38   C. 84   E. 150

    B. 48   D. 169

14) In the figure below, line A is parallel to line B. What is the value of angle x?

    A. 35 degree

    B. 55 degree

    C. 85 degree

    D. 105 degree

    E. 125 degree

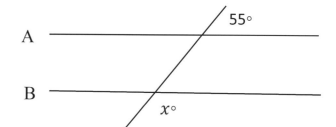

15) Which of the following expressions is equal to $\sqrt{\dfrac{x^2}{3} + \dfrac{x^2}{9}}$?

    A. x C. $x\sqrt{x}$ E. $2x$

    B. $\dfrac{2x}{3}$ D. $\dfrac{x\sqrt{x}}{2}$

16) What is the value of x in the following system of equations?

$$2x + 3y = 10$$
$$6x - 3y = -18$$

A. -1 C. -2 E. 8

B. 1 D. 4

17) An angle is equal to one eighth of its supplement. What is the measure of that angle?

A. 20 C. 45 E. 90

B. 30 D. 60

18) If $sin\alpha = \frac{1}{2}$ in a right triangle and the angle α is an acute angle, then what is $cos\,\alpha$?

A. $\frac{\sqrt{6}}{2}$ C. $\sqrt{3}$ E. $\frac{\sqrt{3}}{2}$

B. $\frac{2}{3}$ D. $\frac{4}{\sqrt{3}}$

19) In the standard (x, y) coordinate system plane, what is the area of the circle with the following equation?

$$(x + 2)^2 + (y - 4)^2 = 9$$

A. 9π C. 4π E. 81

B. 2π D. 3π

20) What are the zeroes of the function $f(x)=x^3+5x^2+6x$?

   A. 0   C. 0, 2, 3   E. 0, $-$ 2, $-$ 3

   B. $-$ 2, $-$ 3   D. $-$ 1, $-$ 3

21) In two successive years, the population of a town is increased by 15% and 20%.

What percent of the population is increased after two years?

   A. 32%   C. 38%   E. 70%

   B. 35%   D. 68%

22) If one angle of a right triangle measures 60°, what is the sine of the other acute

angle?

   A. $\frac{1}{2}$ C. $\frac{\sqrt{3}}{2}$ E. $\sqrt{3}$

   B. $\frac{\sqrt{2}}{2}$ D. 1

23) In the following figure, what is the perimeter of $\Delta\ ABC$ if the area of $\Delta\ ADC$ is

15?

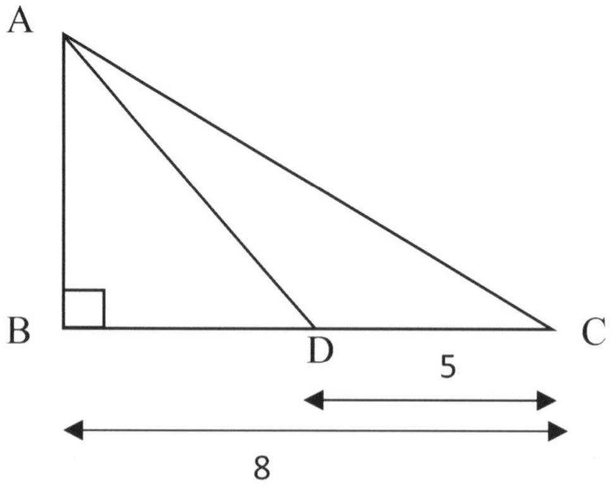

   A. 37.5

   B. 21

   C. 15

   D. 24

   E. The answer cannot be determined from the information given

24) Which of the following is one solution of this equation?

$$x^2 + 2x - 5 = 0$$

A. $\sqrt{2} + 1$ C. $\sqrt{6} - 1$ E. $\sqrt{12}$

B. $\sqrt{2} - 1$ D. $\sqrt{6} + 1$

25) If $x = 9$, what is the value of y in the following equation?

$$3y = \frac{2x^2}{3} + 6$$

A. 20   C. 60   E. 150

B. 35   D. 110

26) A swimming pool holds 3,000 cubic feet of water. The swimming pool is 15 feet long and 10 feet wide. How deep is the swimming pool?

A. 6 feet   C. 8 feet   E. 20 feet

B. 4 feet   D. 10 feet

27) The ratio of boys to girls in a school is 2:6. If there are 800 students in a school, how many boys are in the school.

A. 540   C. 800   E. 200

B. 500   D. 600

28) If $(x - 3)^2 + 1 > 3x - 1$, then x can equal which of the following?

A. 2   C. 8   E. 4

B. 6   D. 3

29) Let r and p be constants. If $x^2 + 4x + r$ factors into $(x + 3)(x + p)$, the values of r and p respectively are?

A. 3, 1

B. 1, 3

C. 2, 3

D. 3, 2

E. The answer cannot be found from the information given.

30) If 120 % of a number is 72, then what is 80 % of that number?

A. 45

B. 50

C. 48

D. 55

E. 80

31) The width of a box is one third of its length. The height of the box is one third of its width. If the length of the box is 36 cm, what is the volume of the box?

A. 144 cm^3

B. 324 cm^3

C. 576 cm^3

D. 1,728 cm^3

E. 2,704 cm^3

32) The average of five consecutive numbers is 36. What is the smallest number?

A. 38

B. 36

C. 34

D. 12

E. 8

33) The surface area of a cylinder is $120\pi\ cm^2$. If its height is 7 cm, what is the radius of the cylinder?

A. 13 cm

B. 11 cm

C. 12 cm

D. 5 cm

E. 7 cm

34) What is the slope of a line that is perpendicular to the line

$$8x - 4y = 16?$$

A. -2

C. 4

E. 14

B. $-\frac{1}{2}$

D. 12

35) What is the difference in area between a 8 cm by 5 cm rectangle and a circle

with diameter of 12 cm? $(\pi = 3)$

A. 56

C. 8

E. 3

B. 68

D. 6

36) If $f(x)=3x^3+ 3$ and $(x) = \frac{1}{x}$, what is the value of $f(g(x))$?

A. $\frac{1}{3x^3+3}$

C. $\frac{1}{3x}$

E. $\frac{3}{x^3} + 3$

B. $\frac{3}{x^3}$

D. $\frac{1}{3x+3}$

37) A cruise line ship left Port A and traveled 50 miles due west and then 120 miles

due north. At this point, what is the shortest distance from the cruise to port A?

A. 70 miles

C. 150 miles

E. 230 miles

B. 80 miles

D. 130 miles

38) The length of a rectangle is 2 meters greater than 3 times its width. The

perimeter of the rectangle is 36 meters. What is the area of the rectangle?

A. 16 m²

C. 56 m²

E. 110 m²

B. 36 m²

D. 72 m²

39) What is the solution of the following inequality?

$$|x - 2| \geq 4$$

A. $x \geq 6 \cup x \leq -2$

D. $x \leq -2$

B. $-2 \leq x \leq 6$

E. Set of real numbers

C. $x \geq 6$

40) In the following figure, ABCD is a rectangle. If $a = \sqrt{3}$, and $b = 4a$, find the area of the shaded region. (the shaded region is a trapezoid)

A. 12

B. 20

C. $10\sqrt{3}$

D. $20\sqrt{3}$

E. $12\sqrt{3}$

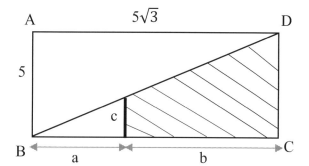

STOP

This is the End of this Test. You may check your work on this Test if you still have time.

DAT Practice Test 3

Quantitative Reasoning

❖ **40 Questions.**

❖ **Total time for this test: 45 Minutes**.

❖ **You may use a basic calculator on this test.**

Administered *Month Year*

1) 124 is equal to?

   A. $20 - (4 \times 10) + (6 \times 30)$

   B. $\left(\frac{11}{8} \times 72\right) + \left(\frac{125}{5}\right)$

   C. $\left(\left(\frac{30}{4} + \frac{13}{2}\right) \times 7\right) - \frac{11}{2} + \frac{110}{4}$

   D. $(2 \times 10) + (50 \times 1.5) + 15$

   E. $\frac{481}{6} + \frac{121}{3}$

2) If $|a| < 2$ then which of the following is true? ($b > 0$)?

   IV. $-2b < ba < 2b$

   V. $-a < a^2 < a \quad if \ a < 0$

   VI. $-7 < 2a - 3 < 1$

   A. I only   C. I and III only   E. I, II and III

   B. II only   D. III only

3) Six years ago, Amy was two times as old as Mike was. If Mike is 14 years old now, how old is Amy?

   A. 34   C. 14   E. 22

   B. 28   D. 20

4) What is the area of a square whose diagonal is 8 cm?

   A. $16 \ cm^2$ C. $36 \ cm^2$ E. $216 \ cm^2$

   B. $32 \ cm^2$ D. $33 \ cm^2$

5) A number is chosen at random from 1 to 10. Find the probability of not selecting a composite number.

A. $\frac{1}{10}$ C. $\frac{2}{5}$ E. 0

B. 10   D. 1

6) Removing which of the following numbers will change the average of the numbers to 6?

$$1, 4, 5, 8, 11, 12$$

A. 11   C. 5   E. 12

B. 4   D. 1

7) A rope weights 600 grams per meter of length. What is the weight in kilograms of 14.2 meters of this rope? (1 kilograms = 1,000 grams)

A. 0.0852   C. 8.52   E. 85,200

B. 0.852   D. 8,520

8) If $y = 4ab + 3b^3$, what is y when $a = 3$ and $b = 1$?

A. 22   C. 24   E. 15

B. 26   D. 12

9) The marked price of a computer is D dollar. Its price decreased by 60% in January and later increased by 10% in February. What is the final price of the computer in D dollar?

A. 0.40 D   C. 0.70 D   E. 1.80 D

B. 0.44 D   D. 1.40 D

10) The number 80.5 is 1,000 times greater than which of the following numbers?

A. 0.805

C. 0.0850

E. 0.000805

B. 0.0805

D. 0.00805

11) David's current age is 44 years, and Ava's current age is 8 years. In how many years David's age will be 4 times Ava's age?

A. 4

C. 8

E. 14

B. 6

D. 10

12) How many tiles of 9 cm² is needed to cover a floor of dimension 8 cm by 36 cm?

A. 15

C. 20

E. 36

B. 18

D. 32

13) What is the value of x in the following figure?

A. 150

B. 175

C. 135

D. 95

E. 105

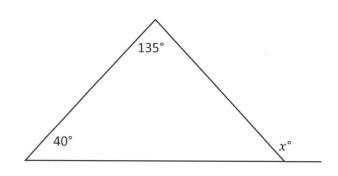

14) Right triangle ABC is shown below. Which of the following is true for all possible values of angle A and B?

A. $\tan A = \tan B$

B. $\tan^2 A = \tan^2 B$

C. $\tan A = 1$

D. $\sin A = \cos B$

E. $\cot A = \sin B$

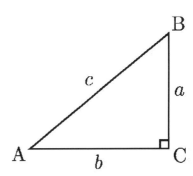

15) What is the value of y in the following system of equation?

$$4x - 3y = -12$$

$$-x + y = 4$$

A. -4

B. -2

C. 8

D. 5

E. 4

16) From the figure, which of the following must be true? (figure not drawn to scale)

A. $y = z$

B. $y = 5x$

C. $y \geq x$

D. $y + 4x = z$

E. $y > x$

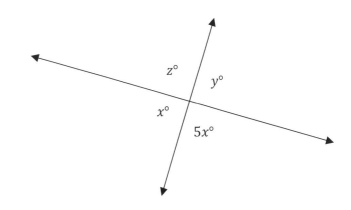

17) When 30% of 80 is added to 18% of 800, the resulting number is:

A. 36　　　　　　　　　C. 168　　　　　　　　　E. 175

B. 95　　　　　　　　　D. 120

18) A ladder leans against a wall forming a 60° angle between the ground and the ladder. If the bottom of the ladder is 40 feet away from the wall, how long is the ladder?

A. 40 feet　　　　　　　C. 50 feet　　　　　　　E. 160 feet

B. 60 feet　　　　　　　D. 80 feet

19) If 80 % of a class are girls, and 15 % of girls play tennis, what percent of the class play tennis?

A. 12 %　　　　　　　　C. 15 %　　　　　　　　E. 60 %

B. 9 %　　　　　　　　D. 30 %

20) If x is a real number, and if $x^3 + 28 = 120$, then x lies between which two consecutive integers?

A. 1 and 2　　　　　　　C. 3 and 4　　　　　　　E. 5 and 6

B. 2 and 3　　　　　　　D. 4 and 5

21) If $(x - 3)^3 = 8$ which of the following could be the value of $(x - 4)(x - 3)$?

A. 1　　　　　　　　　C. 6　　　　　　　　　E. −2

B. 2　　　　　　　　　D. −1

22) In five successive hours, a car travels 40 km, 42 km, 55 km, 38 km and 50 km. In the next five hours, it travels with an average speed of 60 km per hour. Find the total distance the car traveled in 10 hours.

A. 525 km   C. 468 km   E. 1,000 km

B. 430 km   D. 510 km

23) From last year, the price of gasoline has increased from $1.15 per gallon to $1.61 per gallon. The new price is what percent of the original price?

A. 72%   C. 120%   E. 180%

B. 140%   D. 160%

24) If $\tan \theta = \frac{6}{8}$ and $\sin \theta > 0$, then $\cos \theta = ?$

A. $-\frac{4}{5}$ C. $\frac{5}{12}$ E. 0

B. $\frac{4}{5}$ D. $-\frac{12}{5}$

25) Which of the following shows the numbers in increasing order?

A. $\frac{1}{3}, \frac{7}{11}, \frac{4}{7}, \frac{3}{4}$ D. $\frac{7}{11}, \frac{3}{4}, \frac{4}{7}, \frac{1}{3}$

B. $\frac{1}{3}, \frac{4}{7}, \frac{7}{11}, \frac{3}{4}$ E. None of them above

C. $\frac{4}{7}, \frac{3}{4}, \frac{7}{11}, \frac{1}{3}$

26) x is $y\%$ of what number?

A. $\frac{x}{100y}$ C. $\frac{100x}{y}$ E. $\frac{xy}{100}$

B. $\frac{y}{100x}$ D. $\frac{100y}{x}$

27) If cotangent of an angel β is 1, then the tangent of angle β is

   A. −1   C. 0   E. $-\frac{1}{2}$

   B. 1   D. $\frac{1}{2}$

28) If a box contains red and blue balls in ratio of 4: 5, how many red balls are there if 90 blue balls are in the box?

   A. 90   C. 30   E. 8

   B. 72   D. 10

29) 6 liters of water are poured into an aquarium that's 20cm long, 5cm wide, and 50cm high. How many cm will the water level in the aquarium rise due to this added water? (1 liter of water = 1000 cm^3)

   A. 80   C. 50   E. 4

   B. 60   D. 10

30) What is the surface area of the cylinder below?

   A. 40 π in^2

   B. 40 π^{2}in^2

   C. 88 π in^2

   D. 88 π^{2}in^2

   E. 56 π in^2

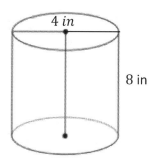

31) A chemical solution contains 3% alcohol. If there is 24ml of alcohol, what is the volume of the solution?

   A. 320 ml   C. 800 ml   E. 1,400 ml

   B. 380 ml   D. 1,300 ml

32) What is the solution of the following inequality?

$$|x - 8| \leq 4$$

A. $x \geq 12 \cup x \leq 8$

D. $x \leq 8$

B. $4 \leq x \leq 12$

E. Set of real numbers

C. $x \geq 12$

33) Which of the following points lies on the line $4x - y = -3$?

A. $(3, -1)$

C. $(-1, 1)$

E. $(0, -3)$

B. $(-1, 3)$

D. $(3, -3)$

34) In the following figure, ABCD is a rectangle, and E and F are points on AD and DC, respectively. The area of ΔBED is 15, and the area of ΔBDF is 20. What is the perimeter of the rectangle?

A. 32

B. 22

C. 20

D. 40

E. 44

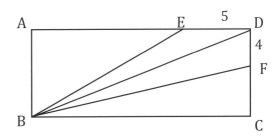

35) In the xy-plane, the point $(5, 7)$ and $(4, 6)$ are online A. Which of the following equations of lines is parallel to line A?

A. $y = 3x$

C. $y = \frac{x}{2}$

E. $y = x$

B. $y = 10$

D. $y = 2x$

36) If $f(x) = 2^x$ and $g(x) = log_2 x$, which of the following expressions is equal to $f(2g(p))$?

A. $2P$ C. p^2 E. $\frac{p}{2}$

B. 2^p D. p^4

37) If a tree casts a 54–foot shadow at the same time that a 5 feet yardstick casts a 3–foot shadow, what is the height of the tree?

A. 16 ft

B. 30 ft

C. 90ft

D. 46 ft

E. 50 ft

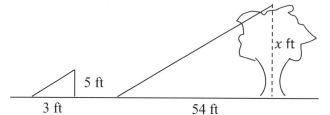

38) If the area of trapezoid is 120, what is the perimeter of the trapezoid?

A. 37

B. 48

C. 53

D. 57

E. 63

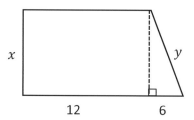

39) In the following equation when z is divided by 5, what is the effect on x?

$$x = \frac{8y + \frac{r}{r+1}}{\frac{10}{z}}$$

A. x is divided by 3   D. x is multiplied by 5

B. x is divided by 5   E. x is multiplied by 3

C. x does not change

40) If 80% of x equal to 20% of 40, then what is the value of $(x + 4)^2$?

A. 12.20

C. 25.01

E. 196

B. 24

D. 1810

STOP

This is the End of this Test. You may check your work on this Test if you still

have time.

DAT Practice Test 4

Quantitative Reasoning

❖ **40 Questions.**

❖ **Total time for this test: 45 Minutes**.

❖ **You may use a basic calculator on this test.**

Administered *Month Year*

1) Convert 640,000 to scientific notation.

   A. 6.40×1000 D. 6.4×10^5

   B. 6.40×10^{-5} E. 6.4×10^4

   C. 6.4×100^2

2) $(x^4)^{\frac{5}{8}}$ equal to?

   A. $x^{\frac{5}{2}}$ C. $x^{\frac{4}{15}}$ E. $x^{\frac{5}{48}}$

   B. $x^{\frac{42}{8}}$ D. $x^{\frac{8}{42}}$

3) The average weight of 30 girls in a class is 60 kg and the average weight of 20 boys in the same class is 65 kg. What is the average weight of all the 50 students in that class?

   A. 60   C. 61.28   E. 62.48

   B. 62   D. 62.90

4) If $y = (-3x^3)^2$, which of the following expressions is equal to y?

   A. $-9x^6$ C. $9x^5$ E. $9x^6$

   B. $-6x^6$ D. $6x^6$

5) Sophia purchased a sofa for $406.25 The sofa is regularly priced at $625. What was the percent discount Sophia received on the sofa?

   A. 15%   C. 20%   E. 40%

   B. 35%   D. 25%

6) What is the value of the expression $2(x - y) + (1 - x)^2$ when $x = 2$ and $= -3$?

A. $- 8$

C. 11

E. 45

B. 18

D. 32

7) If $f(x) = 2x - 5$ and $g(x) = x^2 - 4x$, then find $(\frac{f}{g})(x)$.

A. $\dfrac{2x-5}{x^2-4x}$

C. $\dfrac{x-1}{x^2-1}$

E. $\dfrac{x^2-4x}{2x-5}$

B. $\dfrac{x-1}{x^2-4x}$

D. $\dfrac{2x+1}{x^2+4x}$

8) In the standard (x, y) coordinate plane, which of the following lines contains the points $(3, -5)$ and $(8, 10)$?

A. $y = 3x - 14$

D. $y = -\dfrac{1}{3}x + 14$

B. $y = \dfrac{1}{3}x + 14$

E. $y = 2x - 11$

C. $y = -3x + 7$

9) A bank is offering 2.5% simple interest on a savings account. If you deposit $13,000, how much interest will you earn in two years?

A. $450

C. $4,500

E. $4,600

B. $650

D. $6,400

10) If the interior angles of a quadrilateral are in the ratio 1:3:5:6, what is the measure of the largest angle?

A. 24°

C. 108°

E. 144°

B. 72°

D. 120°

11) If $x + \sin^2 a + \cos^2 a = 4$, then $x = ?$

A. 1   C. 2   E. 5

B. 3   D. 4

12) If the area of a circle is 64 square meters, what is its diameter?

A. 8π C. $\frac{16\sqrt{\pi}}{\pi}$ E. $8\sqrt{\pi}$

B. $\frac{8\sqrt{\pi}}{\pi}$ D. $64\pi^2$

13) The length of a rectangle is $\frac{3}{4}$ times its width. If the width is 32, what is the perimeter of this rectangle?

A. 24   C. 112   E. 150

B. 48   D. 132

14) In the figure below, line A is parallel to line B. What is the value of angle x?

A. 35 degree

B. 45 degree

C. 85 degree

D. 105 degree

E. 135 degree

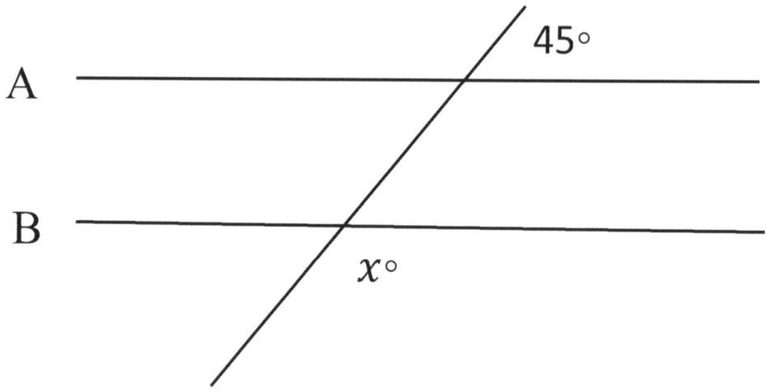

15) Which of the following expressions is equal to $\sqrt{\frac{x^2}{2} + \frac{x^2}{16}}$?

A. x C. $x\sqrt{x}$ E. $2x$

B. $\frac{3x}{4}$ D. $\frac{x\sqrt{x}}{2}$

16) What is the value of x in the following system of equations?

$$2x + 3y = 8$$
$$6x - 3y = -24$$

A. -2 C. -1 E. 4

B. 1   D. 3

17) An angle is equal to one eighth of its supplement. What is the measure of that angle?

A. 20   C. 45   E. 90

B. 30   D. 60

18) If $sin\alpha = \frac{1}{2}$ in a right triangle and the angle α is an acute angle, then what is $cos\ \alpha$?

A. $\frac{\sqrt{6}}{2}$ C. $\sqrt{3}$ E. $\frac{\sqrt{3}}{2}$

B. $\frac{2}{3}$ D. $\frac{4}{\sqrt{3}}$

19) In the standard (x, y) coordinate system plane, what is the area of the circle with the following equation?

$$(x + 2)^2 + (y - 4)^2 = 4$$

A. 94π C. 9π E. 81

B. 2π D. 3π

20) What are the zeroes of the function $f(x) = x^3 + 7x^2 + 12x$?

A. 0

C. 0, 3, 4

E. 0, −3, −4

B. −3, −4

D. −1, −4

21) In two successive years, the population of a town is increased by 25% and 40%.

What percent of the population is increased after two years?

A. 32%

C. 75%

E. 70%

B. 35%

D. 40%

22) If one angle of a right triangle measures 60°, what is the sine of the other acute

angle?

A. $\frac{1}{2}$

C. $\frac{\sqrt{3}}{2}$

E. $\sqrt{3}$

B. $\frac{\sqrt{2}}{2}$

D. 1

23) In the following figure, what is the perimeter of $\Delta\,ABC$ if the area of $\Delta\,ADC$ is

30?

A. 37.5

B. 23

C. 11

D. 48

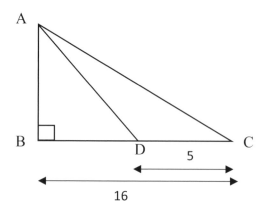

E. The answer cannot be determined from the information given

24) Which of the following is one solution of this equation?

$$2x^2 + 4x - 10 = 0$$

A. $\sqrt{2} + 1$ C. $\sqrt{6} - 1$ E. $\sqrt{12}$

B. $\sqrt{2} - 1$ D. $\sqrt{6} + 1$

25) If $x = 6$, what is the value of y in the following equation?

$$4y = \frac{2x^2}{3} + 8$$

A. 8   C. 60   E. 120

B. 16   D. 110

26) A swimming pool holds 3,600 cubic feet of water. The swimming pool is 12 feet long and 10 feet wide. How deep is the swimming pool?

A. 6 feet   C. 8 feet   E. 30 feet

B. 4 feet   D. 10 feet

27) The ratio of boys to girls in a school is 2:6. If there are 400 students in a school, how many boys are in the school.

A. 540   C. 400   E. 100

B. 250   D. 300

28) If $(x - 3)^2 + 1 > 3x + 1$, then x can equal which of the following?

A. 2   C. 8   E. 4

B. 6   D. 3

29) Let r and p be constants. If $x^2 + 6x + r$ factors into $(x + 5)(x + p)$, the values of r and p respectively are?

A. 5, 1

C. 2, 5

B. 1, 5

D. 5, 2

E. The answer cannot be found from the information given.

30) If 150% of a number is 75, then what is 60% of that number?

A. 45

C. 30

E. 75

B. 50

D. 55

31) The width of a box is one third of its length. The height of the box is one third of its width. If the length of the box is 45 cm, what is the volume of the box?

A. 144 cm^3

C. 576 cm^3

E. 2,704 cm^3

B. 324 cm^3

D. 3,375 cm^3

32) The average of five consecutive numbers is 34. What is the smallest number?

A. 28

C. 32

E. 8

B. 30

D. 12

33) The surface area of a cylinder is $132\pi\ cm^2$. If its height is 5 cm, what is the radius of the cylinder?

A. 13 cm

C. 12 cm

E. 7 cm

B. 11 cm

D. 6 cm

34) What is the slope of a line that is perpendicular to the line $9x - 3y = 18$?

A. -3 C. 6   E. 14

B. $-\frac{1}{3}$ D. 18

35) What is the difference in area between a 9 cm by 5 cm rectangle and a circle with diameter of 16 cm? $(\pi = 3)$

A. 47   C. 9   E. 3

B. 147   D. 6

36) If $f(x) = 4x^3 + 4$ and $g(x) = \frac{1}{x}$, what is the value of $f(g(x))$?

A. $\frac{1}{4x^3 + 4}$ C. $\frac{1}{4x}$ E. $\frac{4}{x^3} + 4$

B. $\frac{4}{x^3}$ D. $\frac{1}{4x + 4}$

37) A cruise line ship left Port A and traveled 50 miles due west and then 120 miles due north. At this point, what is the shortest distance from the cruise to port A?

A. 70 miles   C. 150 miles   E. 230 miles

B. 80 miles   D. 130 miles

38) The length of a rectangle is 2 meters greater than 3 times its width. The perimeter of the rectangle is 36 meters. What is the area of the rectangle?

A. 16 m^2 C. 56 m^2 E. 110 m^2

B. 36 m^2 D. 72 m^2

39) What is the solution of the following inequality?

$$|x - 3| \geq 5$$

A. $x \geq 8 \cup x \leq -2$

D. $x \leq -2$

B. $-2 \leq x \leq 8$

E. Set of real numbers

C. $x \geq 8$

40) In the following figure, ABCD is a rectangle. If $a = \sqrt{3}$, and $b = 4a$, find the area of the shaded region. (the shaded region is a trapezoid)

A. 12

B. 20

C. $10\sqrt{3}$

D. $20\sqrt{3}$

E. $12\sqrt{3}$

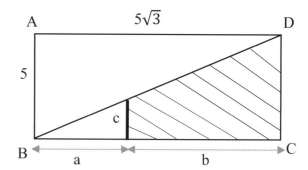

STOP

This is the End of this Test. You may check your work on this Test if you still have time.

DAT Practice Test 5

Quantitative Reasoning

❖ **40 Questions.**

❖ **Total time for this test: 45 Minutes**.

❖ **You may use a basic calculator on this test.**

Administered *Month Year*

1) 121 is equal to?

   A. $25 - (5 \times 8) + (7 \times 20)$

   B. $\left(\frac{10}{7} \times 63\right) + \left(\frac{124}{4}\right)$

   C. $\left(\left(\frac{70}{6} + \frac{22}{33}\right) \times 7\right) - \frac{20}{3} + \frac{130}{6}$

   D. $(3 \times 11) + (42 \times 2.5) + 14$

   E. $\frac{148}{8} + \frac{207}{2}$

2) If $|a| < 3$ then which of the following is true? ($b > 0$)?

   VII. $-3b < ba < 3b$

   VIII. $-a < a^2 < a \quad if \ a < 0$

   IX. $-13 < 3a - 4 < 5$

   A. I only   C. I and III only   E. I, II and III

   B. II only   D. III only

3) Four years ago, Amy was three times as old as Mike was. If Mike is 15 years old now, how old is Amy?

   A. 38   C. 11   E. 37

   B. 22   D. 33

4) What is the area of a square whose diagonal is 12 cm?

   A. 116 cm^2 C. 76 cm^2 E. 36 cm^2

   B. 72 cm^2 D. 38 cm^2

5) A number is chosen at random from 11 to 20. Find the probability of not selecting a composite number.

A. $\frac{1}{20}$ C. $\frac{2}{5}$ E. 0

B. 20   D. 1

6) Removing which of the following numbers will change the average of the numbers to 8?

$$3, 6, 7, 10, 13, 14$$

A. 13   C. 7   E. 14

B. 6   D. 3

7) A rope weights 400 grams per meter of length. What is the weight in kilograms of 13.8 meters of this rope? (1 kilograms = 1,000 grams)

A. 0.0552   C. 5.52   E. 55,200

B. 0.552   D. 5,520

8) If $y = 5ab + 4b^3$, what is y when $a = 2$ and $b = 2$?

A. 20   C. 28   E. 52

B. 58   D. 25

9) The marked price of a computer is D dollar. Its price decreased by 70% in January and later increased by 20% in February. What is the final price of the computer in D dollar?

A. 0.30 D   C. 0.60 D   E. 1.60 D

B. 0.36 D   D. 1.36 D

10) The number 96.4 is 100 times greater than which of the following numbers?

A. 9.640　　　　　C. 0.0964　　　　　E. 0.000964

B. 0.964　　　　　D. 0.00964

11) David's current age is 70 years, and Ava's current age is 10 years. In how many years David's age will be 5 times Ava's age?

A. 5　　　　　C. 9　　　　　E. 15

B. 7　　　　　D. 12

12) How many tiles of 15 cm² is needed to cover a floor of dimension 9 cm by 45 cm?

A. 25　　　　　C. 10　　　　　E. 45

B. 8　　　　　D. 27

13) What is the value of x in the following figure?

A. 160

B. 175

C. 155

D. 90

E. 130

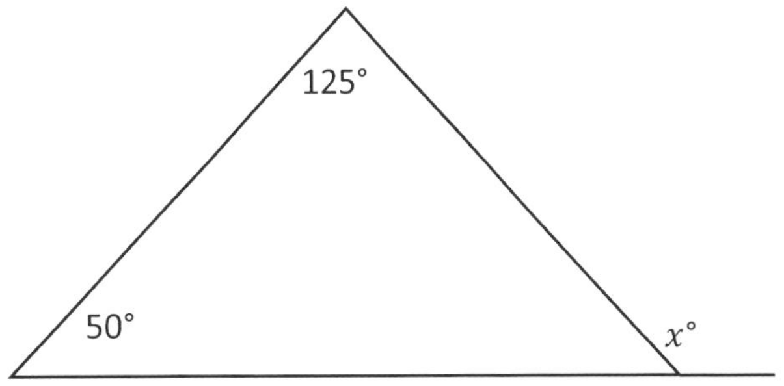

14) Right triangle ABC is shown below. Which of the following is true for all possible values of angle A and B?

A. $\tan A = \tan B$

B. $\tan^2 B = \tan^2 A$

C. $\tan B = 1$

D. $\sin B = \cos A$

E. $\cot B = \sin A$

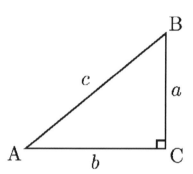

15) What is the value of y in the following system of equation?

$$2x - 5y = -8$$

$$-x + 2y = 3$$

A. -6 C. 7 E. 2

B. -3 D. 4

16) From the figure, which of the following must be true? (figure not drawn to scale)

A. $y = 4z$

B. $y = 6x$

C. $y \geq x$

D. $2y + 5x = z$

E. $y > x$

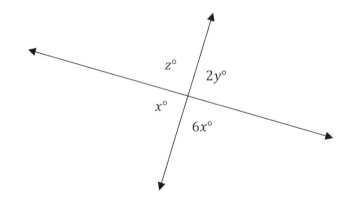

17) When 40% of 70 is added to 15% of 600, the resulting number is:

  A. 28   C. 118   E. 185

  B. 90   D. 128

18) A ladder leans against a wall forming a 60° angle between the ground and the ladder. If the bottom of the ladder is 30 feet away from the wall, how long is the ladder?

  A. 90 feet   C. 30 feet   E. 150 feet

  B. 45 feet   D. 60 feet

19) If 75 % of a class are girls, and 24 % of girls play tennis, what percent of the class play tennis?

  A. 18 %   C. 55 %   E. 40 %

  B. 10 %   D. 24 %

20) If x is a real number, and if $x^2 + 43 = 100$, then x lies between which two consecutive integers?

  A. 5 and 6   C. 4 and 5   E. 3 and 4

  B. 6 and 7   D. 7 and 8

21) If $(x - 5)^3 = 1$ which of the following could be the value of $(x - 5)(x - 2)$?

  A. 5   C. 8   E. -4

  B. 4   D. -5

22) In five successive hours, a car travels 42 km, 44 km, 57 km, 41 km and 52 km. In the next five hours, it travels with an average speed of 56 km per hour. Find the total distance the car traveled in 10 hours.

A. 516 km

B. 416 km

C. 568 km

D. 236 km

E. 280 km

23) From last year, the price of gasoline has increased from $1.25 per gallon to $1.625 per gallon. The new price is what percent of the original price?

A. 70%

B. 130%

C. 150%

D. 170%

E. 160%

24) If $cot\ \theta = \frac{3}{4}$ and $sin\ \theta > 0$, then $sin\ \theta = ?$

A. $-\frac{3}{5}$

B. $\frac{4}{5}$

C. $\frac{5}{13}$

D. $-\frac{13}{5}$

E. 1

25) Which of the following shows the numbers in increasing order?

A. $\frac{1}{2}, \frac{8}{13}, \frac{5}{7}, \frac{2}{5}$

B. $\frac{2}{5}, \frac{1}{2}, \frac{8}{13}, \frac{5}{7}$

C. $\frac{5}{7}, \frac{2}{5}, \frac{8}{13}, \frac{1}{2}$

D. $\frac{2}{5}, \frac{7}{11}, \frac{5}{7}, \frac{1}{2}$

E. None of them above

26) y is $x\%$ of what number?

A. $\frac{y}{100x}$

B. $\frac{x}{100y}$

C. $\frac{100y}{x}$

D. $\frac{100x}{y}$

E. $\frac{xy}{100}$

27) If tangent of an angel β is $\frac{\sqrt{3}}{3}$, then the cotangent of angle β is

A. $\frac{\sqrt{3}}{3}$

B. 0

C. $\sqrt{3}$

D. $\frac{\sqrt{3}}{2}$

E. $-\frac{\sqrt{3}}{3}$

28) If a box contains red and blue balls in ratio of 3: 8, how many red balls are there if 96 blue balls are in the box?

A. 96

B. 36

C. 32

D. 24

E. 11

29) 5 liters of water are poured into an aquarium that's 25cm long, 4cm wide, and 45cm high. How many cm will the water level in the aquarium rise due to this added water? (1 liter of water = 1000 cm³)

A. 100

B. 50

C. 40

D. 20

E. 5

30) What is the surface area of the cylinder below?

A. 60 π in²

B. 60 π² in²

C. 78 π in²

D. 78 π² in²

E. 46 π in²

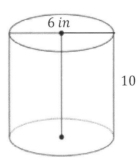

6 in

10

31) A chemical solution contains 7% alcohol. If there is 28ml of alcohol, what is the volume of the solution?

A. 420 ml

B. 340 ml

C. 400 ml

D. 1,000 ml

E. 1,200 ml

32) What is the solution of the following inequality?

$$|x - 7| \leq 3$$

A. $x \geq 10 \cup x \leq 7$

D. $x \leq 7$

B. $4 \leq x \leq 10$

E. Set of real numbers

C. $x \geq 10$

33) Which of the following points lies on the line $5x - 2y = -6$?

A. $(0, -4)$

C. $(-2, -2)$

E. $(2, 0)$

B. $(-3, 1)$

D. $(1, -2)$

34) In the following figure, ABCD is a rectangle, and E and F are points on AD and DC, respectively. The area of ΔBED is 16, and the area of ΔBDF is 25. What is the perimeter of the rectangle?

A. 36

B. 24

C. 40

D. 30

E. 34

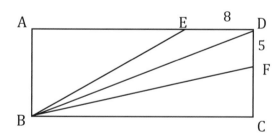

35) In the xy-plane, the point $(3, 9)$ and $(2, 8)$ are online A. Which of the following equations of lines is parallel to line A?

A. $y = 8x$

C. $y = \frac{x}{3}$

E. $y = x$

B. $y = 9$

D. $y = 3x$

36) If $f(x) = 5^x$ and $g(x) = log_5 x$, which of the following expressions is equal to $f(5g(p))$?

A. $5P$

C. p^5

E. $\frac{p}{5}$

B. 5^p

D. $5p^5$

37) If a tree casts a 68–foot shadow at the same time that a 7 feet yardstick casts a 4–foot shadow, what is the height of the tree?

A. 19 ft

B. 88 ft

C. 119ft

D. 56 ft

E. 80 ft

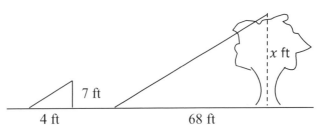

38) If the area of trapezoid is 210, what is the perimeter of the trapezoid?

A. 42

B. 62

C. 52

D. 32

E. 68

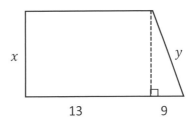

39) In the following equation when z is divided by 6, what is the effect on x?

$$x = \frac{7y + \frac{r}{2r+3}}{\frac{12}{z}}$$

A. x is divided by 2

D. x is multiplied by 6

B. x is divided by 6

E. x is multiplied by 2

C. x does not change

40) If 60% of x equal to 15% of 20, then what is the value of $(x+6)^2$?

A. 11.12

C. 21.15

E. 121

B. 11

D. 1,214

STOP

This is the End of this Test. You may check your work on this Test if you still

have time.

DAT Practice Test 6

Quantitative Reasoning

❖ **40 Questions.**

❖ **Total time for this test: 45 Minutes**.

❖ **You may use a basic calculator on this test.**

Administered *Month Year*

1) Convert 830,000 to scientific notation.

    A. 8.30×1000

    B. 8.30×10^{-5}

    C. 8.3×100^2

    D. 8.3×10^5

    E. 8.3×10^4

2) $(x^5)^{\frac{3}{10}}$ equal to?

    A. $x^{\frac{3}{2}}$

    B. $x^{\frac{2}{3}}$

    C. $x^{\frac{3}{15}}$

    D. $x^{\frac{3}{5}}$

    E. $x^{\frac{5}{3}}$

3) The average weight of 25 girls in a class is 40 kg and the average weight of 15 boys in the same class is 64 kg. What is the average weight of all the 40 students in that class?

    A. 40

    B. 49

    C. 50.5

    D. 50

    E. 45.5

4) If $y = (-2x^2)^4$, which of the following expressions is equal to y?

    A. $-16x^8$

    B. $-16x^6$

    C. $16x^6$

    D. $8x^8$

    E. $16x^8$

5) Sophia purchased a sofa for $399 The sofa is regularly priced at $532. What was the percent discount Sophia received on the sofa?

    A. 45%

    B. 25%

    C. 30%

    D. 75%

    E. 50%

6) What is the value of the expression $4(x + y) + (2 - x)^2$ when $x = 3$ and $y = -1$?

    A. -9 C. 9   E. 22

    B. 19   D. 12

7) If $f(x) = 3x - 7$ and $g(x) = x^3 - 6x$, then find $(\frac{f}{g})(x)$.

    A. $\frac{3x-7}{x^3-6x}$ C. $\frac{x-7}{x^3-1}$ E. $\frac{x^3-6x}{3x-7}$

    B. $\frac{x-7}{x^3-2x}$ D. $\frac{3x+7}{x^3+4x}$

8) In the standard (x, y) coordinate plane, which of the following lines contains the points $(1, -7)$ and $(6, 8)$?

    A. $y = 3x - 10$ D. $y = -\frac{1}{3}x + 10$

    B. $y = \frac{1}{3}x + 10$ E. $y = 2x - 12$

    C. $y = -3x + 8$

9) A bank is offering 1.5% simple interest on a savings account. If you deposit $12,000, how much interest will you earn in four years?

    A. $360   C. $7,200   E. $5,600

    B. $720   D. $3,600

10) If the interior angles of a quadrilateral are in the ratio 1:2:7:8, what is the measure of the largest angle?

    A. 20°   C. 110°   E. 160°

    B. 40°   D. 140°

11) If $x + 2sin^2a + 2cos^2a = 6$, then $x =$?

    A. 3   C. 8   E. 0

    B. 4   D. 6

12) If the area of a circle is 81 square meters, what is its diameter?

    A. 9π C. $\dfrac{18\sqrt{\pi}}{\pi}$ E. $9\sqrt{\pi}$

    B. $\dfrac{9\sqrt{\pi}}{\pi}$ D. $81\pi^2$

13) The length of a rectangle is $\dfrac{2}{5}$ times its width. If the width is 25, what is the perimeter of this rectangle?

    A. 10   C. 75   E. 150

    B. 25   D. 100

14) In the figure below, line A is parallel to line B. What is the value of angle x?

    A. 30 degree

    B. 40 degree

    C. 150 degree

    D. 100 degree

    E. 130 degree

15) Which of the following expressions is equal to $\sqrt{\dfrac{3x^2}{5} + \dfrac{x^2}{25}}$?

    A. $5x$ C. $x\sqrt{x}$ E. $4x$

    B. $\dfrac{4x}{5}$ D. $\dfrac{x\sqrt{x}}{5}$

16) What is the value of x in the following system of equations?

$$x + 2y = 7$$
$$4x + 5y = 22$$

A. 3   C. -3 E. 6

B. 2   D. 5

17) An angle is equal to one ninth of its supplement. What is the measure of that angle?

A. 18   C. 15   E. 120

B. 36   D. 45

18) If $sin\alpha = \frac{\sqrt{3}}{2}$ in a right triangle and the angle α is an acute angle, then what is $cos\,\alpha$?

A. $\frac{\sqrt{2}}{2}$ C. $\sqrt{2}$ E. $\frac{\sqrt{3}}{3}$

B. $\frac{1}{2}$ D. $\frac{3}{\sqrt{3}}$

19) In the standard (x, y) coordinate system plane, what is the area of the circle with the following equation?

$$(x + 3)^2 + (y - 5)^2 = 9$$

A. 9π C. 6π E. 18

B. 4π D. 2π

20) What are the zeroes of the function $f(x)=x^3+12x^2+32x$?

    A. 0   C. 0, 3, 8   E. $0, -4, -8$

    B. $-4, -8$ D. $-1, -8$

21) In two successive years, the population of a town is increased by 20% and 35%.

    What percent of the population is increased after two years?

    A. 42%   C. 62%   E. 45%

    B. 65%   D. 60%

22) If one angle of a right triangle measures 30°, what is the sine of the other acute

    angle?

    A. $\frac{\sqrt{3}}{2}$ C. $\frac{1}{2}$ E. $\sqrt{3}$

    B. $\frac{\sqrt{2}}{2}$ D. 0

23) In the following figure, what is the perimeter of $\Delta\,ABC$ if the area of $\Delta\,ADC$ is 60?

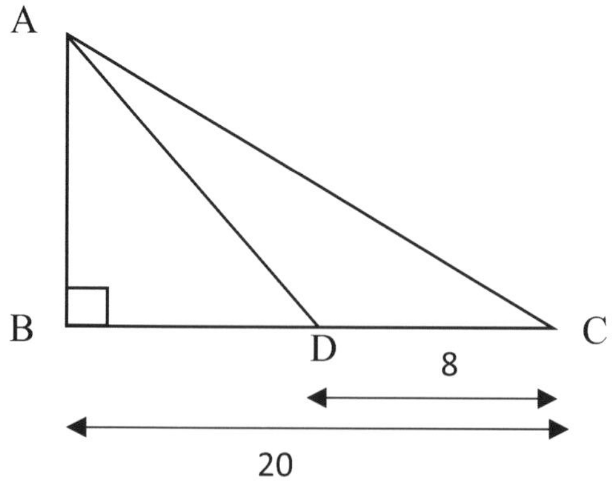

    A. 28

    B. 20

    C. 15

    D. 60

    E. The answer cannot be determined from the information given

24) Which of the following is one solution of this equation?

$$3x^2 + 5x - 8 = 0$$

A. $\sqrt{5} + 1$

C. 1

E. $\sqrt{15}$

B. $\sqrt{5} - 1$

D. $\sqrt{5}$

25) If $x = 4$, what is the value of y in the following equation?

$$5y = \frac{3x^2}{8} + 9$$

A. 3

C. 65

E. 130

B. 15

D. 11

26) A swimming pool holds 5,400 cubic feet of water. The swimming pool is 15 feet long and 12 feet wide. How deep is the swimming pool?

A. 15 feet

C. 10 feet

E. 30 feet

B. 12 feet

D. 20 feet

27) The ratio of boys to girls in a school is 3:5. If there are 480 students in a school, how many boys are in the school.

A. 580

C. 480

E. 180

B. 280

D. 380

28) If $(x - 2)^2 + 3 > 2x + 3$, then x can equal which of the following?

A. 1

C. 7

E. 3

B. 5

D. 2

29) Let r and p be constants. If $x^2 + 4x + r$ factors into $(x + 3)(x + p)$, the values of r and p respectively are?

A. 3, 1

C. 2, 3

B. 1, 3

D. 3, 2

E. The answer cannot be found from the information given.

30) If 200% of a number is 80, then what is 70% of that number?

A. 44

C. 28

E. 40

B. 20

D. 25

31) The width of a box is half of its length. The height of the box is half of its width. If the length of the box is 36 cm, what is the volume of the box?

A. 328 cm³

C. 583 cm³

E. 2,832 cm³

B. 832 cm³

D. 5,832 cm³

32) The average of three consecutive numbers is 42. What is the smallest number?

A. 24

C. 41

E. 42

B. 34

D. 14

33) The surface area of a cylinder is $88\pi\ cm^2$. If its height is 7 cm, what is the radius of the cylinder?

A. 7 cm

C. 8 cm

E. 11 cm

B. 14 cm

D. 4 cm

34) What is the slope of a line that is perpendicular to the line $12x - 4y = 24$?

A. -6 C. 24 E. 4

B. $-\frac{1}{3}$ D. 12

35) What is the difference in area between a 8 cm by 6 cm rectangle and a circle with diameter of 12 cm? ($\pi = 3$)

A. 40 C. 48 E. 6

B. 60 D. 8

36) If $f(x) = 5x^2 + 8$ and $g(x) = \frac{1}{2x}$, what is the value of $f(g(x))$?

A. $\frac{5}{4x^2 + 8}$ C. $\frac{1}{4x}$ E. $\frac{5}{4x^2} + 8$

B. $\frac{4}{x^2}$ D. $\frac{8}{4x + 8}$

37) A cruise line ship left Port A and traveled 60 miles due west and then 80 miles due north. At this point, what is the shortest distance from the cruise to port A?

A. 48 miles   C. 140 miles   E. 200 miles

B. 90 miles   D. 100 miles

38) The length of a rectangle is 5 meters greater than 7 times its width. The perimeter of the rectangle is 58 meters. What is the area of the rectangle?

A. $18 \ m^2$ C. $78 \ m^2$ E. $114 \ m^2$

B. $29 \ m^2$ D. $58 \ m^2$

39) What is the solution of the following inequality?

$$|x - 4| \geq 6$$

A. $x \geq 10 \cup x \leq -2$

D. $x \leq -4$

B. $-2 \leq x \leq 10$

E. Set of real numbers

C. $x \geq 10$

40) In the following figure, ABCD is a rectangle. If $a = \sqrt{2}$, and $b = 2a$, find the area of the shaded region. (the shaded region is a trapezoid)

A. 10

B. 12

C. $9\sqrt{2}$

D. $6\sqrt{2}$

E. $4\sqrt{2}$

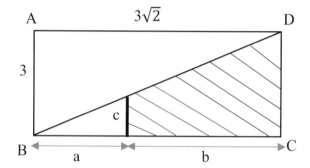

STOP

This is the End of this Test. You may check your work on this Test if you still have time.

Answer Keys

DAT Math Practice Tests

✻ Now, it's time to review your results to see where you went wrong and what

areas you need to improve!

Practice Test 1					
1	B	16	D	31	C
2	C	17	C	32	B
3	E	18	D	33	C
4	B	19	A	34	A
5	C	20	D	35	E
6	A	21	B	36	C
7	C	22	A	37	C
8	E	23	B	38	B
9	B	24	B	39	B
10	B	25	B	40	E
11	A	26	C		
12	D	27	C		
13	B	28	B		
14	D	29	B		
15	E	30	C		

Practice Test 2					
1	D	16	A	31	D
2	A	17	A	32	C
3	B	18	E	33	D
4	E	19	A	34	B
5	B	20	C	35	B
6	C	21	E	36	E
7	A	22	A	37	D
8	A	23	D	38	C
9	B	24	C	39	A
10	E	25	A	40	E
11	B	26	E		
12	C	27	E		
13	C	28	C		
14	E	29	A		
15	B	30	C		

Practice Test 3

1	B	16	D	31	C
2	C	17	C	32	B
3	E	18	D	33	C
4	B	19	A	34	A
5	C	20	D	35	E
6	A	21	B	36	C
7	C	22	A	37	C
8	E	23	B	38	B
9	B	24	B	39	B
10	B	25	B	40	E
11	A	26	C		
12	D	27	C		
13	B	28	B		
14	D	29	B		
15	E	30	C		

Practice Test 4

1	D	16	A	31	D
2	A	17	A	32	C
3	B	18	C	33	D
4	E	19	A	34	B
5	B	20	E	35	B
6	C	21	C	36	E
7	A	22	A	37	D
8	A	23	D	38	C
9	B	24	C	39	A
10	E	25	A	40	E
11	B	26	E		
12	C	27	E		
13	C	28	C		
14	E	29	A		
15	B	30	C		

Practice Test 5

1	B	16	D	31	C
2	C	17	C	32	B
3	E	18	D	33	C
4	B	19	A	34	A
5	C	20	D	35	E
6	A	21	B	36	C
7	C	22	A	37	C
8	E	23	B	38	B
9	B	24	B	39	B
10	B	25	B	40	E
11	A	26	C		
12	D	27	C		
13	B	28	B		
14	D	29	B		
15	E	30	C		

Practice Test 6

1	D	16	A	31	D
2	A	17	A	32	C
3	B	18	B	33	D
4	E	19	A	34	B
5	B	20	E	35	B
6	C	21	C	36	E
7	A	22	A	37	D
8	A	23	D	38	C
9	B	24	C	39	A
10	E	25	A	40	E
11	B	26	E		
12	C	27	E		
13	C	28	C		
14	E	29	A		
15	B	30	C		

Answers and Explanations

Answers and Explanations

DAT Mathematics

Practice Tests 1

1) Answer: B.

Simplify each option provided.

A. $20 - (4 \times 10) + (6 \times 30) = 20 - 40 + 180 = 160$

B. $\left(\frac{11}{8} \times 72\right) + \left(\frac{125}{5}\right) = 99 + 25 = 124$ (this is the answer)

C. $\left(\left(\frac{30}{4} + \frac{13}{2}\right) \times 7\right) - \frac{11}{2} + \frac{110}{4} = \left(\left(\frac{30+26}{4}\right) \times 7\right) - \frac{11}{2} + \frac{55}{2} = \left(\left(\frac{56}{4}\right) \times 7\right) + \frac{55-11}{2} =$

$(14 \times 7) + \frac{44}{2} = 98 + 22 = 120$

D. $(2 \times 10) + (50 \times 1.5) + 15 = 20 + 75 + 15 = 110$

E. $\frac{481}{6} + \frac{121}{3} = \frac{481+242}{6} = 120.5$

2) Answer: C.

I. $|a| < 2 \rightarrow -2 < a < 2$

Multiply all sides by b. Since, $b > 0 \rightarrow -2b < ba < 2b$ (it is true!)

II. Since, $-2 < a < 2, and\ a < 0 \rightarrow -a > a^2 > a$ (plug in $-\frac{1}{2}$, and check!) (It's

false)

III. $-2 < a < 2, multiply\ all\ sides\ by\ 2, then: -4 < 2a < 4$

Subtract 3 from all sides. Then:

$-4 - 3 < 2a - 3 < 2 - 3 \rightarrow -7 < 2a - 3 < 1$ (It is true!)

3) Answer: E.

six years ago, Amy was two times as old as Mike. Mike is 14 years

now. Therefore, 6 years ago Mike was 8 years.

Six years ago, Amy was: $A = 2 \times 8 = 16$

Now Amy is 22 years old: $16 + 6 = 22$

4) Answer: B.

The diagonal of the square is 6. Let x be the side.

Use Pythagorean Theorem: $a^2 + b^2 = c^2$

$x^2 + x^2 = 6^2 \Rightarrow 2x^2 = 6^2 \Rightarrow 2x^2 = 36 \Rightarrow x^2 = 18 \Rightarrow x = \sqrt{18}$

The area of the square is: $\sqrt{18} \times \sqrt{18} = 18$

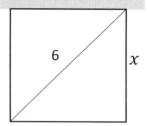

5) Answer: C.

Set of number that are not composite between 1 and 15: A= {1,2, 3, 5, 7, 11, 13}

Probability $= \dfrac{number\ of\ desired\ outcomes}{number\ of\ total\ outcomes} = \dfrac{7}{15}$

6) Answer: A.

Check each option provided:

A. 1 $\dfrac{4+5+8+11+12}{5} = \dfrac{40}{5} = 8$

B. 4 $\dfrac{1+5+8+11+12}{5} = \dfrac{37}{5} = 7.4$

C. 5 $\dfrac{1+4+8+11+12}{5} = \dfrac{36}{5} = 7.2$

D. 11 $\dfrac{1+4+5+8+12}{5} = \dfrac{30}{5} = 6$

E. 12 $\dfrac{1+4+5+8+11}{5} = \dfrac{29}{5} = 5.8$

7) Answer: C.

The weight of 13.2 meters of this rope is: 13.2 × 700 g = 9,240 g

1 kg = 1,000 g, therefore, 9,240 g ÷ 1000 = 9.24 kg

8) Answer: E.

$y = 5ab + 2b^3$

Plug in the values of a and b in the equation: $a = 3$ and $b = 1$

$y = 5\ (3)\ (1) + 2\ (1)^3 = 15 + 2(1) = 15 + 2 = 17$

9) Answer: B.

To find the discount, multiply the number by (100% – rate of discount).

Therefore, for the first discount we get: (D) (100% – 40%) = (D) (0.60) = 0.60 D

For increase of 10 %: (0.60 D) (100% + 10%) = (0.60 D) (1.10) = 0.66 D = 66% of D

10) Answer: B.

1,000 times the number is 60.5. Let x be the number, then:

$1,000x = 60.5 \rightarrow x = \frac{60.5}{1,000} = 0.0605$

11) Answer: A.

Let's review the options provided.

A. 4. In 4 years, David will be 48 and Ava will be 12. 48 is 4 times 12.

B. 6. In 6 years, David will be 50 and Ava will be 14. 50 is NOT 4 times 14!

C. 8. In 8 years, David will be 52 and Ava will be 16. 52 is not 4 times 16.

D. 10. In 10 years, David will be 54 and Ava will be 18. 54 is not 4 times 18.

E. 14. In 14 years, David will be 58 and Ava will be 22. 58 is not 4 times 20.

12) Answer: D.

The area of the floor is: $7 \text{ cm} \times 32 \text{ cm} = 224 \text{ cm}$

The number is tiles needed $= 224 \div 8 = 28$

13) Answer: B.

$x = 30 + 135 = 165$

14) Answer: D.

By definition, the sine of any acute angle is equal to the cosine of its complement.

Since, angle A and B are complementary angles, therefore:

$sin\, A = cos\, B$

15) Answer: E.

Solve the system of equations by elimination method.

$\begin{array}{l} 4x - 2y = -20 \\ -x + y = 10 \end{array}$ Multiply the second equation by 4, then add it to the first equation.

$\begin{array}{l} 4x - 2y = -20 \\ 4(-x + y = 10) \end{array} \Rightarrow \begin{array}{l} 4x - 2y = -20 \\ -4x + 4y = 40) \end{array} \Rightarrow$ add the equations

$2y = 20 \Rightarrow y = 10$

16) Answer: D.

x and z are colinear. y and $4x$ are colinear. Therefore,

$x + z = y + 4x, subtract\ x\ from\ both\ sides, then, z = y + 3x$

17) Answer: C.

30% of 80 equals to: $0.30 \times 80 = 24$

18% of 800 equals to: $0.18 \times 800 = 144$

30% of 40 is added to 18% of 800: $24 + 144 = 168$

18) Answer: D.

The relationship among all sides of special right triangle

$30° - 60° - 90°$ is provided in this triangle:

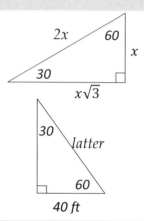

In this triangle, the opposite side of 30° angle is half of the

hypotenuse. Draw the shape of this question.

The latter is the hypotenuse.

Therefore, the latter is 80 ft.

19) Answer: A.

The percent of girls playing tennis is: $60\% \times 15\% = 0.60 \times 0.15 = 0.090 = 9\%$

20) Answer: D.

Solve for x. $x^3 + 18 = 140 \Rightarrow x^3 = 122$

Let's review the options.

  A. 1 and 2. $1^3 = 1$ and $2^3 = 8$, 122 is not between these two numbers.

  B. 2 and 3. $2^3 = 8$ and $3^3 = 27$, 122 is not between these two numbers.

  C. 3 and 4. $3^3 = 27$ and $4^3 = 64$, 122 is not between these two numbers.

  D. 4 and 5. $4^3 = 64$ and $5^3 = 125$, 122 is between these two numbers.

  E. 5 and 6. $5^3 = 125$ and $6^3 = 216$, 122 is not between these two numbers.

21) Answer: B.

$(x - 2)^3 = 8 \rightarrow x - 2 = 2 \rightarrow x = 4$

$\rightarrow (x - 3)(x - 2) = (4 - 3)(4 - 2) = (1)(2) = 2$

22) Answer: A.

Add the first 5 numbers. $40 + 42 + 55 + 38 + 50 = 225$

To find the distance traveled in the next 5 hours, multiply the average by number of

hours.

Distance = Average × Rate = 60 × 5 = 300

Add both numbers. 300 + 225 = 525

23) Answer: B.

The question is this: 1.38 is what percent of 1.15

Use percent formula: $part = \frac{percent}{100} \times whole$

$1.38 = \frac{percent}{100} \times 1.15 \Rightarrow 1.38 = \frac{percent \times 1.15}{100} \Rightarrow 138 = percent \times 1.15 \Rightarrow percent = \frac{138}{1.15}$

$= 120$

24) Answer: B.

$tan\theta = \frac{opposite}{adjacent}$

$tan\theta = \frac{3}{4} \Rightarrow$ we have the following right triangle. Then,

$c = \sqrt{3^2 + 4^2} = \sqrt{9 + 16} = \sqrt{25} = 5$

$cos\theta = \frac{adjacent}{hypotenuse} = \frac{4}{5}$

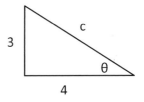

25) Answer: B.

$\frac{1}{3} \cong 0.33$ $\frac{4}{7} \cong 0.57$ $\frac{7}{11} \cong 0.63$ $\frac{3}{4} = 0.75$

26) Answer: C.

Let the number be A. Then:

$x = y\% \times A \rightarrow$ (Solve for A)$\rightarrow x = \frac{y}{100} \times A$

Multiply both sides by $\frac{100}{y}$: $x \times \frac{100}{y} = \frac{y}{100} \times \frac{100}{y} \times A$

$A = \frac{100x}{y}$

27) Answer: C.

$tangent\ \beta = \frac{1}{cotangent\ \beta} = \frac{1}{1} = 1$

28) Answer: B.

$\frac{3}{4} \times 80 = 60$

29) Answer: B.

One liter=1,000 cm³→ 4 liters=4,000 cm^3

$4,000 = 20 \times 5 \times h \to h = \frac{4,000}{100} = 40$ cm

30) Answer: C.

Surface Area of a cylinder $= 2\pi r \,(r + h)$,

The radius of the cylinder is 2 (4÷ 2) inches and its height is 7 inches. Therefore,

Surface Area of a cylinder $= 2\pi \,(2)\,(2 + 7) = 36\,\pi$

31) Answer: C.

3% of the volume of the solution is alcohol. Let x be the volume of the solution.

Then: 3% of $x = 21$ml $\Rightarrow 0.03\,x = 21 \Rightarrow x = 21 \div 0.03 = 700$

32) Answer: B.

$|x - 8| \leq 2 \to -2 \leq x - 8 \leq 2 \to -2 + 8 \leq x - 8 + 8 \leq 2 + 8 \to 6 \leq x \leq 10$

33) Answer: C.

Plug in each pair of number in the equation:

   A. $(3, -1)$: $4\,(3) - (-1) = 13$ Nope!

   B. $(-1, 3)$: $4\,(-1) - (3) = -7$ Nope!

   C. $(-1, -1)$: $4\,(-1) - (-1) = -3$ Bingo!

   D. $(3, -3)$: $4\,(3) - (-3) = 15$ Nope!

   E. $(0, -3)$: $4\,(0) - (-3) = 3$ Nope!

34) Answer: A.

The area of ΔBED is 10, then: $\frac{5 \times AB}{2} = 10 \to 5 \times AB = 20 \to AB = 4$

The area of ΔBDF is 12, then: $\frac{4 \times BC}{2} = 12 \to 4 \times BC = 24 \to BC = 6$

The perimeter of the rectangle is $= 2 \times (4 + 6) = 20$

35) Answer: E.

The slop of line A is: $m = \frac{y_2 - y_1}{x_2 - x_1} = \frac{6-5}{5-4} = 1$

Parallel lines have the same slope and only choice E (y = x) has slope of 1.

36) Answer: C.

To solve for $f(2g(P))$, first, find $2g(p)$

$g(x) = log_2 x \rightarrow g(p) = log_2 p \rightarrow 2g(p) = 2log_2 p = log_2 p^2$

Now, find $f(2g(p))$: $f(x) = 2^x \rightarrow f(log_2 p^2) = 2^{log_2 p^2}$

Logarithms and exponentials with the same base cancel each other. This is true because logarithms and exponentials are inverse operations. Then: $f(log_2 p^2) = 2^{log_2 p^2} = p^2$

37) Answer: C.

Write a proportion and solve for x.

$\frac{5}{3} = \frac{x}{48} \Rightarrow 3x = 5 \times 48 \Rightarrow x = 80$ ft

38) Answer: B.

The area of trapezoid is: $\left(\frac{9+15}{2}\right) \times x = 96 \rightarrow 12x = 96 \rightarrow x = 8$

$y = \sqrt{8^2 + 6^2} = 10$

Perimeter is: $15 + 8 + 9 + 10 = 42$

39) Answer: B.

$x_1 = \frac{8y + \frac{r}{r+1}}{\frac{10}{\frac{z}{5}}} = \frac{8y + \frac{r}{r+1}}{\frac{5 \times 10}{z}} = \frac{8y + \frac{r}{r+1}}{5 \times \frac{10}{z}} = \frac{1}{5} \times \frac{8y + \frac{r}{r+1}}{10} = \frac{x}{5}$

40) Answer: E.

$0.6x = (0.2) \times 30 \rightarrow x = 10 \rightarrow (x+2)^2 = (12)^2 = 144$

Answers and Explanations

DAT Mathematics

Practice Tests 2

1) Answer: D.

$840,000 = 8.4 \times 10^5$

2) Answer: A.

$(x^6)^{\frac{5}{8}} = x^{6 \times \frac{5}{8}} = x^{\frac{30}{8}} = x^{\frac{15}{4}}$

3) Answer: B.

$\text{average} = \dfrac{\text{sum of terms}}{\text{number of terms}}$

The sum of the weight of all girls is: $20 \times 60 = 1,200$ kg

The sum of the weight of all boys is: $30 \times 65 = 1,950$ kg

The sum of the weight of all students is: $1,080 + 1,984 = 3,150$ kg

$\text{average} = \dfrac{3,150}{50} = 63$

4) Answer: E.

$y = (-2x^3)^2 = (-2)^2(x^3)^2 = 4x^6$

5) Answer: B.

The question is this: 399.75 is what percent of 615?

Use percent formula: $\text{part} = \dfrac{\text{percent}}{100} \times \text{whole}$

$399.75 = \dfrac{\text{percent}}{100} \times 615 \Rightarrow 399.75 = \dfrac{\text{percent} \times 615}{100} \Rightarrow 39,975 = \text{percent} \times 615 \Rightarrow \text{percent}$

$= \dfrac{39,975}{615} = 65$

399.75 is 65 % of 615. Therefore, the discount is: $100\% - 65\% = 35\%$

6) Answer: C.

Plug in the value of x and y.

$x = 3$ and $y = -4$

$3(x - y) + (1 - x)^2 = 3(3 - (-4)) + (1 - 3)^2 = 3(3 + 4) + (-2)^2 = 21 + 4 = 25$

7) Answer: A.

$$\left(\frac{f}{g}\right)(x) = \frac{f(x)}{g(x)} = \frac{2x-1}{x^2-2x}$$

8) Answer: A.

The equation of a line is: $y = mx + b$, where m is the slope and b is the y-intercept.

First find the slope: $m = \frac{y_2 - y_1}{x_2 - x_1} = \frac{10-(-5)}{8-3} = \frac{15}{5} = 3$

Then, we have: $y = 3x + b$

Choose one point and plug in the values of x and y in the equation to solve for b.

Let's choose the point $(3, -5)$

$y = 3x + b \rightarrow -5 = 3(3) + b \rightarrow -5 = 9 + b \rightarrow b = -14$

The equation of the line is: $y = 3x - 14$

9) Answer: B.

Use simple interest formula: $I = prt$ (I = interest, p = principal, r = rate, t = time)

$I = (15,000)(0.025)(2) = 750$

10) Answer: E.

The sum of all angles in a quadrilateral is 360 degrees.

Let x be the smallest angle in the quadrilateral. Then the angles are: $x, 2x, 4x, 5x$

$x + 2x + 4x + 5x = 360 \rightarrow 12x = 360 \rightarrow x = 30$

The angles in the quadrilateral are: $30°, 60°, 120°,$ and $150°$

11) Answer: B.

$sin^2 a + cos^2 a = 1$, then: $x + 1 = 3 \rightarrow x = 2$

12) Answer: C.

Formula for the area of a circle is: $A = \pi r^2$

Using 81 for the area of the circle we have: $81 = \pi r^2$

Let's solve for the radius (r). $\frac{81}{\pi} = r^2 \rightarrow r = \sqrt{\frac{81}{\pi}} = \frac{9}{\sqrt{\pi}} = \frac{9}{\sqrt{\pi}} \times \frac{\sqrt{\pi}}{\sqrt{\pi}} = \frac{9\sqrt{\pi}}{\pi}$

13) Answer: C.

Length of the rectangle is: $\frac{3}{4} \times 24 = 18$

perimeter of rectangle is: $2 \times (18 + 24) = 84$

14) Answer: E.

The angle x and 55 are complementary angles. Therefore:

$x + 55 = 180 \Rightarrow 180° - 55° = 125°$

15) Answer: B.

Simplify the expression.

$$\sqrt{\frac{x^2}{3} + \frac{x^2}{9}} = \sqrt{\frac{3x^2}{9} + \frac{x^2}{9}} = \sqrt{\frac{4x^2}{9}} = \sqrt{\frac{4}{9}x^2} = \sqrt{\frac{4}{9}} \times \sqrt{x^2} = \frac{2}{3} \times x = \frac{2x}{3}$$

16) Answer: A.

Solving Systems of Equations by Elimination

Multiply the first equation by (–3), then add it to the second equation.

$$\begin{array}{r} -3(2x + 3y = 10) \\ 6x - 3y = -18 \end{array} \Rightarrow \begin{array}{r} -6x - 9y = -30 \\ 6x - 3y = -18 \end{array} \Rightarrow -12y = -48 \Rightarrow y = 4$$

Plug in the value of y into one of the equations and solve for x.

$2x + 3(4) = 10 \Rightarrow 2x + 12 = 10 \Rightarrow 2x = -2 \Rightarrow x = -1$

17) Answer: A.

The sum of supplement angles is 180. Let x be that angle. Therefore, $x + 8x = 180 \Rightarrow 9x = 180$, divide both sides by 9: $x = 20$

18) Answer: E.

$sin\alpha = \frac{1}{2} \Rightarrow$ Since $sin\alpha = \frac{opposite}{hypotenuse}$, we have the following right triangle. Then,

$c = \sqrt{4^2 - 2^2} = \sqrt{16 - 4} = \sqrt{12}$

$cos\alpha = \frac{\sqrt{12}}{4} = \frac{\sqrt{4} \times \sqrt{3}}{4} = \frac{\sqrt{3}}{2}$

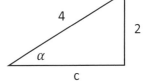

19) Answer: A.

The equation of a circle in standard form is:

$(x - h)^2 + (y - k)^2 = r^2$, where r is the radius of the circle.

In this circle the radius is 9. $r^2 = 9 \rightarrow r = 3$

$(x + 2)^2 + (y - 4)^2 = 9$

Area of a circle: $A = \pi r^2 = \pi(3)^2 = 9\pi$

20) Answer: E.

Frist factor the function: $f(x) = x^3 + 5x^2 + 6x = x(x+2)(x+3)$

To find the zeros, $f(x)$ should be zero. $f(x) = x(x+2)(x+3) = 0$

Therefore, the zeros are: $x = 0$

$(x+2) = 0 \Rightarrow x = -2$; $(x+3) = 0 \Rightarrow x = -3$

21) Answer: C.

the population is increased by 15% and 20%. 15% increase changes the population to 115% of original population.

For the second increase, multiply the result by 120%.

$(1.15) \times (1.20) = 1.38 = 138\%$

38 percent of the population is increased after two years.

22) Answer: A.

The relationship among all sides of right triangle $30° - 60° - 90°$ is provided in the following triangle:

Sine of 30° equals to: $\dfrac{opposite}{hypotenuse} = \dfrac{x}{2x} = \dfrac{1}{2}$

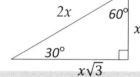

23) Answer: D.

Let x be the length of AB, then: $15 = \dfrac{x \times 5}{2} \rightarrow x = 6$

The length of $AC = \sqrt{6^2 + 8^2} = \sqrt{100} = 10$

The perimeter of $\Delta ABC = 6 + 8 + 10 = 24$

24) Answer: C.

$x_{1,2} = \dfrac{-b \pm \sqrt{b^2 - 4ac}}{2a}$

$ax^2 + bx + c = 0 \Rightarrow x^2 + 2x - 5 = 0$, then: a = 1, b = 2 and c = − 5

$x = \dfrac{-2 + \sqrt{2^2 - 4.1.-5}}{2.1} = \sqrt{6} - 1$; $x = \dfrac{-2 - \sqrt{2^2 - 4.1.-5}}{2.1} = -1 - \sqrt{6}$

25) Answer: A.

Plug in the value of x in the equation and solve for y.

$3y = \frac{2x^2}{3} + 6 \rightarrow 3y = \frac{2(9)^2}{3} + 6 \rightarrow 3y = \frac{2(81)}{3} + 6 \rightarrow 3y = 54 + 6 = 60 \rightarrow 3y = 60 \rightarrow y = 20$

26) Answer: E.

Use formula of rectangle prism volume.

$V = (\text{length}) (\text{width}) (\text{height}) \Rightarrow 3{,}000 = (15)(10)(\text{height}) \Rightarrow \text{height} = 3{,}000 \div 150 = 20$

27) Answer: E.

Th ratio of boy to girls is 2:6. Therefore, there are 2 boys out of 8 students. To find the answer, first divide the total number of students by 8, then multiply the result by 2.

$800 \div 8 = 100 \Rightarrow 100 \times 2 = 200$

28) Answer: C.

Plug in the value of each option in the inequality.

A. $2(2-3)^2 + 1 > 3(1) - 1 \rightarrow 2 > 2$ No!

B. $6(6-3)^2 + 1 > 3(6) - 1 \rightarrow 10 > 17$ No!

C. $8(8-3)^2 + 1 > 3(8) - 1 \rightarrow 26 > 23$ Bingo!

D. $3(3-3)^2 + 1 > 3(3) - 1 \rightarrow 1 > 8$ No!

E. $4(4-3)^2 + 1 > 3(4) - 1 \rightarrow 2 > 11$ No!

29) Answer: A.

$(x+3)(x+p) = x^2 + (3+p)x + 3p \rightarrow 3 + p = 4 \rightarrow p = 1 \ and \ r = 3p = 3$

30) Answer: C.

First, find the number. Let x be the number. Write the equation and solve for x.

120 % of a number is 72, then:

$1.2 \times x = 72 \Rightarrow x = 72 \div 1.2 = 60$

80 % of 60 is: $0.8 \times 60 = 48$

31) Answer: D.

If the length of the box is 36, then the width of the box is one third of it, 12, and the height of the box is 4 (one third of the width). The volume of the box is:

$V = (\text{length}) \times (\text{width}) \times (\text{height}) = (36) \times (12) \times (4) = 1{,}728$

32) Answer: C.

Let x be the smallest number. Then, these are the numbers:

$x, x + 1, x + 2, x + 3, x + 4$

average $= \dfrac{\text{sum of terms}}{\text{number of terms}} \Rightarrow 36 = \dfrac{x+(x+1)+(x+2)+(x+3)+(x+4)}{5} \Rightarrow 36 = \dfrac{5x+10}{5} \Rightarrow 180 =$

$5x + 10 \Rightarrow 170 = 5x \Rightarrow x = 34$

33) Answer: D.

Formula for the Surface area of a cylinder is: $SA = 2\pi r^2 + 2\pi rh$

$\to 120\pi = 2\pi r^2 + 2\pi r(7) \to r^2 + 7r - 60 = 0$

Factorize and solve for r.

$(r + 12)(r - 5) = 0 \to r = 5 \quad or \quad r = -12$ (unacceptable)

34) Answer: B.

The equation of a line in slope intercept form is: $y = mx + b$

Solve for y.

$8x - 4y = 16 \Rightarrow -4y = 16 - 8x \Rightarrow y = (16 - 8x) \div (-4) \Rightarrow$

$y = 2x - 4 \to$ The slope is 2.

The slope of the line perpendicular to this line is:

$m_1 \times m_2 = -1 \Rightarrow 2 \times m_2 = -1 \Rightarrow m_2 = -\dfrac{1}{2}$

35) Answer: B.

The area of rectangle is: $8 \times 5 = 40$ cm²

The area of circle is: $\pi r^2 = \pi \times (\dfrac{12}{2})^2 = 3 \times 36 = 108 \ cm^2$

Difference of areas is: $108 - 40 = 68$

36) Answer: E.

$f\big(g(x)\big) = 3 \times (\dfrac{1}{x})^3 + 3 = \dfrac{3}{x^3} + 3$

37) Answer: D.

Use the information provided in the question to draw

the shape. Use Pythagorean Theorem: $a^2 + b^2 = c^2$

$50^2 + 120^2 = c^2 \Rightarrow 2,500 + 14,400 = c^2$

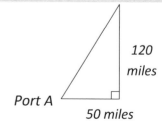

Port A

120 miles

50 miles

$\Rightarrow 16,900 = c^2 \Rightarrow c = 130$

38) Answer: C.

Let L be the length of the rectangular and W be the with of the rectangular. Then, $L = 3W + 2$

The perimeter of the rectangle is 36 meters. Therefore:

$2L + 2W = 36 \Rightarrow L + W = 18$

Replace the value of L from the first equation into the second equation and solve for

$W: (3W + 2) + W = 18 \to 4W + 2 = 18 \to 4W = 16 \to W = 4$

The width of the rectangle is 4 meters and its length is:

$L = 3W + 2 = 3(4) + 2 = 14$

The area of the rectangle is: length × width $= 14 \times 4 = 56$

39) Answer: A.

$x - 2 \geq 4 \to x \geq 4 + 2 \to x \geq 6$

Or $x - 2 \leq -4 \to x \leq -4 + 2 \to x \leq -2$

Then, solution is: $x \geq 6 \cup x \leq -2$

40) Answer: E.

Based on triangle similarity theorem:

$\frac{a}{a+b} = \frac{c}{5} \to c = \frac{5a}{a+b} = \frac{5\sqrt{3}}{\sqrt{3}+4\sqrt{3}} = 1$

$\to$ area of shaded region is: $\left(\frac{c+5}{2}\right)(b) = 3 \times 4\sqrt{3} = 12\sqrt{3}$

Answers and Explanations

DAT Mathematics

Practice Tests 3

1) Answer: B.

Simplify each option provided.

A. $20 - (4 \times 10) + (6 \times 30) = 20 - 40 + 180 = 160$

B. $\left(\frac{11}{8} \times 72\right) + \left(\frac{125}{5}\right) = 99 + 25 = 124$ (this is the answer)

C. $\left(\left(\frac{30}{4} + \frac{13}{2}\right) \times 7\right) - \frac{11}{2} + \frac{110}{4} = \left(\left(\frac{30+26}{4}\right) \times 7\right) - \frac{11}{2} + \frac{55}{2} = \left(\left(\frac{56}{4}\right) \times 7\right) + \frac{55-11}{2} =$

$(14 \times 7) + \frac{44}{2} = 98 + 22 = 120$

D. $(2 \times 10) + (50 \times 1.5) + 15 = 20 + 75 + 15 = 110$

E. $\frac{481}{6} + \frac{121}{3} = \frac{481+242}{6} = 120.5$

2) Answer: C.

I. $|a| < 2 \rightarrow -2 < a < 2$

Multiply all sides by b. Since, $b > 0 \rightarrow -2b < ba < 2b$ (it is true!)

II. Since, $-2 < a < 2,$ and $a < 0 \rightarrow -a > a^2 > a$ (plug in $-\frac{1}{2}$, and check!) (It's false)

III. $-2 < a < 2,$ multiply all sides by $2,$ then: $-4 < 2a < 4$

Subtract 3 from all sides. Then:

$-4 - 3 < 2a - 3 < 2 - 3 \rightarrow -7 < 2a - 3 < 1$ (It is true!)

3) Answer: E.

six years ago, Amy was two times as old as Mike. Mike is 14 years now. Therefore, 6 years ago Mike was 8 years.

Six years ago, Amy was: $A = 2 \times 8 = 16$

Now Amy is 22 years old: $16 + 6 = 22$

4) Answer: B.

The diagonal of the square is 8. Let x be the side.

Use Pythagorean Theorem: $a^2 + b^2 = c^2$

$x^2 + x^2 = 8^2 \Rightarrow 2x^2 = 8^2 \Rightarrow 2x^2 = 64 \Rightarrow x^2 = 32 \Rightarrow x = \sqrt{32}$

The area of the square is: $\sqrt{32} \times \sqrt{32} = 32$

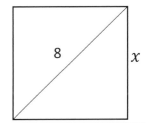

5) Answer: C.

Set of number that are not composite between 1 and 10: A= {2, 3, 5, 7}

Probability $= \dfrac{number\ of\ desired\ outcomes}{number\ of\ total\ outcomes} = \dfrac{4}{10} = \dfrac{2}{5}$

6) Answer: A.

Check each option provided:

A. 11 $\dfrac{1+4+5+8+12}{5} = \dfrac{30}{5} = 6$

B. 4 $\dfrac{1+5+8+11+12}{5} = \dfrac{37}{5} = 7.4$

C. 5 $\dfrac{1+4+8+11+12}{5} = \dfrac{36}{5} = 7.2$

D. 1 $\dfrac{4+5+8+11+12}{5} = \dfrac{40}{5} = 8$

E. 12 $\dfrac{1+4+5+8+11}{5} = \dfrac{29}{5} = 5.8$

7) Answer: C.

The weight of 14.2 meters of this rope is: 14.2×600 g $= 8,520$ g

1 kg = 1,000 g, therefore, 8,520 g ÷ 1,000 = 8.52 kg

8) Answer: E.

$y = 4ab + 3b^3$

Plug in the values of a and b in the equation: $a = 3$ and $b = 1$

$y = 4\,(3)\,(1) + 3\,(1)^3 = 12 + 3(1) = 12 + 3 = 15$

9) Answer: B.

To find the discount, multiply the number by (100% – rate of discount).

Therefore, for the first discount we get: (D) (100% – 60%) = (D) (0.40) = 0.40 D

For increase of 10 %: (0.40 D) (100% + 10%) = (0.40 D) (1.10) = 0.44 D = 44% of D

10) Answer: B.

1,000 times the number is 80.5. Let x be the number, then:

$$1,000x = 80.5 \rightarrow x = \frac{80.5}{1,000} = 0.0805$$

11) Answer: A.

Let's review the options provided.

A. 4. In 4 years, David will be 48 and Ava will be 12. 48 is 4 times 12.

B. 6. In 6 years, David will be 50and Ava will be 14. 50 is NOT 4 times 14.

C. 8. In 8 years, David will be 52 and Ava will be 16. 52 is not 4 times 16.

D. 10. In 10 years, David will be 54 and Ava will be 18. 54 is not 4 times 18.

E. 14. In 14 years, David will be 58 and Ava will be 22. 58 is not 4 times 20.

12) Answer: D.

The area of the floor is: $8 \text{ cm} \times 36 \text{ cm} = 288 \text{ cm}^2$

The number is tiles needed $= 288 \div 9 = 32$

13) Answer: B.

$$x = 40 + 135 = 175$$

14) Answer: D.

By definition, the sine of any acute angle is equal to the cosine of its complement.

Since, angle A and B are complementary angles, therefore:

$$\sin A = \cos B$$

15) Answer: E.

Solve the system of equations by elimination method.

$\begin{aligned} 4x - 3y &= -12 \\ -x + y &= 4 \end{aligned}$ Multiply the second equation by 4, then add it to the first equation.

$\begin{aligned} 4x - 3y &= -12 \\ 4(-x + y &= 4) \end{aligned} \Rightarrow \begin{aligned} 4x - 3y &= -12 \\ -4x + 4y &= 16) \end{aligned} \Rightarrow$ add the equations, $y = 4$

16) Answer: D.

x and z are colinear. y and $5x$ are colinear. Therefore,

$$x + z = y + 5x, subtract\ x\ from\ both\ sides, then, z = y + 4x$$

17) Answer: C.

30% of 80 equals to: $0.30 \times 80 = 24$

18% of 800 equals to: $0.18 \times 800 = 144$

30% of 40 is added to 18% of 800: $24 + 144 = 168$

18) Answer: D.

The relationship among all sides of special right triangle

$30°, \ 60°, \ 90°$ is provided in this triangle:

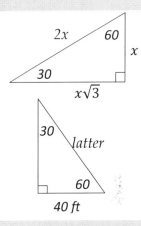

In this triangle, the opposite side of 30° angle is half of the

hypotenuse. Draw the shape of this question.

The latter is the hypotenuse.

Therefore, the latter is 80 ft.

19) Answer: A.

The percent of girls playing tennis is: $80\% \times 15\% = 0.80 \times 0.15 = 0.12 = 12\%$

20) Answer: D.

Solve for x. $x^3 + 28 = 120 \Longrightarrow x^3 = 92$

Let's review the options.

A. 1 and 2. $1^3 = 1$ and $2^3 = 8$, 92 is not between these two numbers.

B. 2 and 3. $2^3 = 8$ and $3^3 = 27$, 92 is not between these two numbers.

C. 3 and 4. $3^3 = 27$ and $4^3 = 64$, 92 is not between these two numbers.

D. 4 and 5. $4^3 = 64$ and $5^3 = 125$, 92 is between these two numbers.

E. 5 and 6. $5^3 = 125$ and $6^3 = 216$, 92 is not between these two numbers.

21) Answer: B.

$(x - 3)^3 = 8 \rightarrow x - 3 = 2 \rightarrow x = 5$

$\rightarrow (x - 4)(x - 3) = (5 - 4)(5 - 3) = (1)(2) = 2$

22) Answer: A.

Add the first 5 numbers. $40 + 42 + 55 + 38 + 50 = 225$

To find the distance traveled in the next 5 hours, multiply the average by number of

hours.

Distance = Average × Rate = 60 × 5 = 300

Add both numbers. 300 + 225 = 525

23) Answer: B.

The question is this: 1.61 is what percent of 1.15

Use percent formula: $part = \frac{percent}{100} \times whole$

$1.61 = \frac{percent}{100} \times 1.15 \Rightarrow 1.61 = \frac{percent \times 1.15}{100} \Rightarrow 161 = percent \times 1.15 \Rightarrow percent = \frac{161}{1.15} = 140$

24) Answer: B.

$tan\theta = \frac{opposite}{adjacent}$

$tan\theta = \frac{6}{8} \Rightarrow$ we have the following right triangle. Then,

$c = \sqrt{6^2 + 8^2} = \sqrt{36 + 64} = \sqrt{100} = 10$

$cos\theta = \frac{adjacent}{hypotenuse} = \frac{8}{10} = \frac{4}{5}$

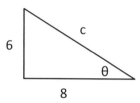

25) Answer: B.

$\frac{1}{3} \cong 0.33 \quad \frac{4}{7} \cong 0.57 \quad \frac{7}{11} \cong 0.64 \quad \frac{3}{4} = 0.75$

26) Answer: C.

Let the number be A. Then:

$x = y\% \times A \rightarrow$ (Solve for A)$\rightarrow x = \frac{y}{100} \times A$

Multiply both sides by $\frac{100}{y}$: $x \times \frac{100}{y} = \frac{y}{100} \times \frac{100}{y} \times A$

$A = \frac{100x}{y}$

27) Answer: C.

$tangent\ \beta = \frac{1}{cotangent\ \beta} = \frac{1}{1} = 1$

28) Answer: B.

$\frac{4}{5} \times 90 = 72$

29) Answer: B.

One liter=1000 cm³→ 6 liters=6,000 cm^3

$6,000 = 20 \times 5 \times h \rightarrow h = \frac{6,000}{100} = 60$ cm

30) Answer: C.

Surface Area of a cylinder = $2\pi r\,(r + h)$,

The radius of the cylinder is 2 ($4 \div 2$) inches and its height is 8 inches. Therefore,

Surface Area of a cylinder = $2\pi\,(2)\,(2 + 8) = 40\,\pi$

31) Answer: C.

3% of the volume of the solution is alcohol. Let x be the volume of the solution.

Then: 3% of x = 24ml $\Rightarrow$ 0.03 x = 24 $\Rightarrow$ x = 24 ÷ 0.03 = 800

32) Answer: B.

$|x - 8| \leq 4 \rightarrow -4 \leq x - 8 \leq 4 \rightarrow -4 + 8 \leq x - 8 + 8 \leq 4 + 8 \rightarrow 4 \leq x \leq 12$

33) Answer: C.

Plug in each pair of number in the equation:

A. $(3, -1)$: $4\,(3) - (-1) = 13$ Nope!

B. $(-1, 3)$: $4\,(-1) - (3) = -7$ Nope!

C. $(-1, -1)$: $4\,(-1) - (-1) = -3$ Bingo!

D. $(3, -3)$: $4\,(3) - (-3) = 15$ Nope!

E. $(0, -3)$: $4\,(0) - (-3) = 3$ Nope!

34) Answer: A.

The area of ΔBED is 15, then: $\frac{5 \times AB}{2} = 15 \rightarrow 5 \times AB = 30 \rightarrow AB = 6$

The area of ΔBDF is 20, then: $\frac{4 \times BC}{2} = 20 \rightarrow 4 \times BC = 40 \rightarrow BC = 10$

The perimeter of the rectangle is = $2 \times (6 + 10) = 32$

35) Answer: E.

The slop of line A is: $m = \frac{y_2 - y_1}{x_2 - x_1} = \frac{7 - 6}{5 - 4} = 1$

Parallel lines have the same slope and only choice E ($y = x$) has slope of 1.

36) Answer: C.

To solve for $f(2g(P))$, first, find $2g(p)$

$g(x) = log_2x \rightarrow g(p) = log_2p \rightarrow 2g(p) = 2log_2p = log_2p^2$

Now, find $f(2g(p))$: $f(x) = 2^x \rightarrow f(log_2p^2) = 2^{log_2p^2}$

Logarithms and exponentials with the same base cancel each other. This is true because logarithms and exponentials are inverse operations. Then: $f(log_2p^2) = 2^{log_2p^2} = p^2$

37) Answer: C.

Write a proportion and solve for x.

$\frac{5}{3} = \frac{x}{54} \Rightarrow 3x = 5 \times 54 \Rightarrow x = 90$ ft

38) Answer: B.

The area of trapezoid is: $\left(\frac{12+18}{2}\right) \times x = 120 \rightarrow 15x = 120 \rightarrow x = 8$

$y = \sqrt{8^2 + 6^2} = 10$

Perimeter is: $18 + 8 + 12 + 10 = 48$

39) Answer: B.

$x_1 = \frac{8y+\frac{r}{r+1}}{\frac{10}{\frac{z}{5}}} = \frac{8y+\frac{r}{r+1}}{\frac{5\times10}{z}} = \frac{8y+\frac{r}{r+1}}{5\times\frac{10}{z}} = \frac{1}{5} \times \frac{8y+\frac{r}{r+1}}{\frac{10}{z}} = \frac{x}{5}$

40) Answer: E.

$0.8x = (0.2) \times 40 \rightarrow x = 10 \rightarrow (x + 4)^2 = (14)^2 = 196$

Answers and Explanations

DAT Mathematics

Practice Tests 4

1) Answer: D.

$640,000 = 6.4 \times 10^5$

2) Answer: A.

$(x^4)^{\frac{5}{8}} = x^{4 \times \frac{5}{8}} = x^{\frac{20}{8}} = x^{\frac{5}{2}}$

3) Answer: B.

$$\text{average} = \frac{\text{sum of terms}}{\text{number of terms}}$$

The sum of the weight of all girls is: $30 \times 60 = 1{,}800$ kg

The sum of the weight of all boys is: $20 \times 65 = 1{,}300$ kg

The sum of the weight of all students is: $1{,}800 + 1{,}300 = 3{,}100$ kg

$$\text{average} = \frac{3{,}100}{50} = 62$$

4) Answer: E.

$y = (-3x^3)^2 = (-3)^2 (x^3)^2 = 9x^6$

5) Answer: B.

The question is this: 406.25 is what percent of 625?

Use percent formula: $\text{part} = \dfrac{\text{percent}}{100} \times \text{whole}$

$406.25 = \dfrac{\text{percent}}{100} \times 625 \Rightarrow 406.25 = \dfrac{\text{percent} \times 625}{100} \Rightarrow 40{,}625 = \text{percent} \times 625 \Rightarrow \text{percent}$

$= \dfrac{40{,}625}{625} = 65$

406.25 is 65% of 625. Therefore, the discount is: $100\% - 65\% = 35\%$

6) Answer: C.

Plug in the value of x and y. $x = 2$ and $y = -3$

$2(x - y) + (1 - x)^2 = 2(2 - (-3)) + (1 - 2)^2 = 2(2 + 3) + (-1)^2 = 11$

7) Answer: A.

$$\left(\frac{f}{g}\right)(x) = \frac{f(x)}{g(x)} = \frac{2x - 5}{x^2 - 4x}$$

8) Answer: A.

The equation of a line is: $y = mx + b$, where m is the slope and b is the y-intercept.

First find the slope: $m = \frac{y_2 - y_1}{x_2 - x_1} = \frac{10 - (-5)}{8 - 3} = \frac{15}{5} = 3$

Then, we have: $y = 3x + b$

Choose one point and plug in the values of x and y in the equation to solve for b.

Let's choose the point $(3, -5)$

$$y = 3x + b \rightarrow -5 = 3(3) + b \rightarrow -5 = 9 + b \rightarrow b = -14$$

The equation of the line is: $y = 3x - 14$

9) Answer: B.

Use simple interest formula:

$I = prt$ (I = interest, p = principal, r = rate, t = time)

$$I = (13,000)(0.025)(2) = 650$$

10) Answer: E.

The sum of all angles in a quadrilateral is 360 degrees.

Let x be the smallest angle in the quadrilateral. Then the angles are: $x, 3x, 5x, 6x$

$$x + 3x + 5x + 6x = 360 \rightarrow 15x = 360 \rightarrow x = 24$$

The angles in the quadrilateral are: $24°$, $72°$, $120°$, and $144°$

11) Answer: B.

$sin^2 a + cos^2 a = 1$, then:

$$x + 1 = 4 \rightarrow x = 3$$

12) Answer: C.

Formula for the area of a circle is: $A = \pi r^2$

Using 64 for the area of the circle we have: $64 = \pi r^2$

Let's solve for the radius (r).

$$\frac{64}{\pi} = r^2 \rightarrow r = \sqrt{\frac{64}{\pi}} = \frac{8}{\sqrt{\pi}} = \frac{8}{\sqrt{\pi}} \times \frac{\sqrt{\pi}}{\sqrt{\pi}} = \frac{8\sqrt{\pi}}{\pi} \rightarrow d = 2r = 2 \times \frac{8\sqrt{\pi}}{\pi} \rightarrow d = \frac{16\sqrt{\pi}}{\pi}$$

13) Answer: C.

Length of the rectangle is: $\frac{3}{4} \times 32 = 24$

perimeter of rectangle is: $2 \times (24 + 32) = 112$

14) Answer: E.

The angle x and 45 are complementary angles. Therefore:

$x + 45 = 180 \Longrightarrow 180° - 45° = 135°$

15) Answer: B.

Simplify the expression.

$\sqrt{\frac{x^2}{2} + \frac{x^2}{16}} = \sqrt{\frac{8x^2}{16} + \frac{x^2}{16}} = \sqrt{\frac{9x^2}{16}} = \sqrt{\frac{9}{16}x^2} = \sqrt{\frac{9}{16}} \times \sqrt{x^2} = \frac{3}{4} \times x = \frac{3x}{4}$

16) Answer: A.

Solving Systems of Equations by Elimination

Multiply the first equation by (–3), then add it to the second equation.

$\begin{array}{l} -3(2x + 3y = 8) \\ \underline{6x - 3y = -24} \end{array} \Rightarrow \begin{array}{l} -6x - 9y = -24 \\ 6x - 3y = -24 \end{array} \Rightarrow -12y = -48 \Rightarrow y = 4$

Plug in the value of y into one of the equations and solve for x.

$2x + 3(4) = 8 \Rightarrow 2x + 12 = 8 \Rightarrow 2x = -4 \Rightarrow x = -2$

17) Answer: A.

The sum of supplement angles is 180. Let x be that angle. Therefore, $x + 8x = 180 \Rightarrow 9x = 180$, divide both sides by 9: $x = 20$

18) Answer: C.

$sin\alpha = \frac{1}{2} \Rightarrow$ Since $sin\alpha = \frac{opposite}{hypotenuse}$, we have the following right triangle. Then,

$c = \sqrt{8^2 - 4^2} = \sqrt{64 - 16} = \sqrt{48}$

$cos\alpha = \frac{\sqrt{48}}{4} = \frac{\sqrt{16} \times \sqrt{3}}{4} = \sqrt{3}$

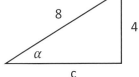

19) Answer: A.

The equation of a circle in standard form is:

$(x - h)^2 + (y - k)^2 = r^2$, where r is the radius of the circle.

In this circle the radius is 4. $r^2 = 4 \rightarrow r = 2$

$(x + 2)^2 + (y - 4)^2 = 2^2$

Area of a circle: $A = \pi r^2 = \pi (2)^2 = 4\pi$

20) Answer: E.

Frist factor the function: $f(x) = x^3 + 7x^2 + 12x = x(x + 3)(x + 4)$

To find the zeros, $f(x)$ should be zero. $f(x) = x(x + 3)(x + 4) = 0$

Therefore, the zeros are: $x = 0$

$(x + 3) = 0 \Rightarrow x = -3 \,;\, (x + 4) = 0 \Rightarrow x = -4$

21) Answer: C.

the population is increased by 25% and 40%. 25% increase changes the population to 125% of original population.

For the second increase, multiply the result by 140%.

$(1.25) \times (1.40) = 1.75 = 175\%$

75 percent of the population is increased after two years.

22) Answer: A.

The relationship among all sides of right triangle $30° - 60° - 90°$ is provided in the following triangle:

Sine of 30° equals to: $\dfrac{opposite}{hypotenuse} = \dfrac{x}{2x} = \dfrac{1}{2}$

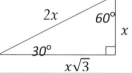

23) Answer: D.

Let x be the length of AB, then: $30 = \dfrac{x \times 5}{2} \rightarrow x = 12$

The length of $AC = \sqrt{12^2 + 16^2} = \sqrt{400} = 20$

The perimeter of $\Delta ABC = 12 + 16 + 20 = 48$

24) Answer: C.

$x_{1,2} = \dfrac{-b \pm \sqrt{b^2 - 4ac}}{2a}$

$ax^2 + bx + c = 0 \Rightarrow 2x^2 + 4x - 10 = 0$, then: a = 2, b = 4 and c = − 10

$x_1 = \dfrac{-4 + \sqrt{4^2 - 4.2. - 10}}{2.2} = \sqrt{6} - 1 \,;\, x_2 = \dfrac{-4 - \sqrt{4^2 - 4.2. - 10}}{2.2} = -1 - \sqrt{6}$

25) Answer: A.

Plug in the value of x in the equation and solve for y.

$$4y = \frac{2x^2}{3} + 8 \rightarrow 4y = \frac{2(6)^2}{3} + 8 \rightarrow 4y = \frac{2(36)}{3} + 8 \rightarrow 4y = 24 + 8 = 32$$

$$\rightarrow 4y = 32 \rightarrow y = 8$$

26) Answer: E.

Use formula of rectangle prism volume.

V = (length) (width) (height) $\Rightarrow$ 3,600 = (12) (10) (height) $\Rightarrow$ height = 3,600 ÷120 = 30

27) Answer: E.

The ratio of boy to girls is 2:6. Therefore, there are 2 boys out of 8 students. To find

the answer, first divide the total number of students by 8, then multiply the result by 2.

400 ÷ 8 = 50 $\Rightarrow$ 50 × 2 = 100

28) Answer: C.

Plug in the value of each option in the inequality.

A. 2: $(2 - 3)^2 + 1 > 3(2) + 1 \rightarrow 2 > 7$ No!

B. 6: $(6 - 3)^2 + 1 > 3(6) + 1 \rightarrow 10 > 19$ No!

C. 8: $(8 - 3)^2 + 1 > 3(8) + 1 \rightarrow 26 > 25$ Bingo!

D. 3: $(3 - 3)^2 + 1 > 3(3) + 1 \rightarrow 1 > 10$ No!

E. 4: $(4 - 3)^2 + 1 > 3(4) + 1 \rightarrow 2 > 13$ No!

29) Answer: A.

$(x + 5)(x + p) = x^2 + (5 + p)x + 5p \rightarrow 5 + p = 6 \rightarrow p = 1 \ and \ r = 5p = 5$

30) Answer: C.

First, find the number.

Let x be the number. Write the equation and solve for x.

150% of a number is 75, then:

$1.5 \times x = 75 \Rightarrow x = 75 \div 1.5 = 50$

60% of 50 is: $0.6 \times 50 = 30$

31) Answer: D.

If the length of the box is 45, then the width of the box is one third of it, 15, and the

height of the box is 5 (one third of the width). The volume of the box is:

V = (length) × (width) × (height) = (45) × (15) × (5) = 3,375

32) Answer: C.

Let x be the smallest number. Then, these are the numbers:

$x, x + 1, x + 2, x + 3, x + 4$

average $= \dfrac{\text{sum of terms}}{\text{number of terms}} \Rightarrow 34 = \dfrac{x+(x+1)+(x+2)+(x+3)+(x+4)}{5} \Rightarrow 34 = \dfrac{5x+10}{5} \Rightarrow 170 =$

$5x + 10 \Rightarrow 160 = 5x \Rightarrow x = 32$

33) Answer: D.

Formula for the Surface area of a cylinder is: $SA = 2\pi r^2 + 2\pi rh$

$\rightarrow 132\pi = 2\pi r^2 + 2\pi r(5) \rightarrow r^2 + 5r - 66 = 0$

Factorize and solve for r.

$$(r + 11)(r - 6) = 0 \rightarrow r = 6 \quad or \quad r = -11 \ (unacceptable)$$

34) Answer: B.

The equation of a line in slope intercept form is: $y = \text{m}x + b$

Solve for y.

$9x - 3y = 18 \Rightarrow -3y = 18 - 9x \Rightarrow y = (18 - 9x) \div (-3) \Rightarrow$

$y = 3x - 6 \rightarrow$ The slope is 3.

The slope of the line perpendicular to this line is:

$m_1 \times m_2 = -1 \Rightarrow 3 \times m_2 = -1 \Rightarrow m_2 = -\dfrac{1}{3}$

35) Answer: B.

The area of rectangle is: $9 \times 5 = 45 \ cm^2$

The area of circle is: $\pi r^2 = \pi \times (\frac{16}{2})^2 = 3 \times 64 = 192 \ cm^2$

Difference of areas is: $192 - 45 = 147$

36) Answer: E.

$f\big(g(x)\big) = 4 \times (\frac{1}{x})^3 + 4 = \dfrac{4}{x^3} + 4$

37) Answer: D.

Use the information provided in the question to draw

the shape. Use Pythagorean Theorem: $a^2 + b^2 = c^2$

$50^2 + 120^2 = c^2 \Rightarrow 2{,}500 + 14{,}400 = c^2$

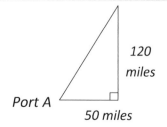

Port A

120 miles

50 miles

$\Rightarrow 16,900 = c^2 \Rightarrow c = 130$

38) Answer: C.

Let L be the length of the rectangular and W be the with of the rectangular. Then, $L = 3W + 2$

The perimeter of the rectangle is 36 meters. Therefore:

$2L + 2W = 36 \Rightarrow L + W = 18$

Replace the value of L from the first equation into the second equation and solve for

$W: (3W + 2) + W = 18 \rightarrow 4W + 2 = 18 \rightarrow 4W = 16 \rightarrow W = 4$

The width of the rectangle is 4 meters and its length is:

$L = 3W + 2 = 3(4) + 2 = 14$

The area of the rectangle is: length × width = $14 \times 4 = 56$

39) Answer: A.

$x - 3 \geq 5 \rightarrow x \geq 5 + 3 \rightarrow x \geq 8$

Or $x - 3 \leq -5 \rightarrow x \leq -5 + 3 \rightarrow x \leq -2$

Then, solution is: $\quad x \geq 8 \ \cup \ x \leq -2$

40) Answer: E.

Based on triangle similarity theorem:

$\frac{a}{a+b} = \frac{c}{5} \rightarrow c = \frac{5a}{a+b} = \frac{5\sqrt{3}}{\sqrt{3}+4\sqrt{3}} = 1$

$\rightarrow$ area of shaded region is: $\left(\frac{c+5}{2}\right)(b) = 3 \times 4\sqrt{3} = 12\sqrt{3}$

Answers and Explanations

DAT Mathematics

Practice Tests 5

1) Answer: B.

Simplify each option provided.

A. $25 - (5 \times 8) + (7 \times 20) = 25 - 40 + 140 = 125$

B. $\left(\frac{10}{7} \times 63\right) + \left(\frac{124}{4}\right) = 90 + 31 = 121$ (this is the answer)

C. $\left(\left(\frac{70}{6} + \frac{22}{3}\right) \times 5\right) - \frac{20}{3} + \frac{130}{6} = \left(\left(\frac{70+44}{6}\right) \times 5\right) - \frac{40}{6} + \frac{130}{6} = \left(\left(\frac{114}{6}\right) \times 5\right) +$

$\frac{130-40}{6} = (19 \times 5) + \frac{90}{6} = 95 + 15 = 110$

D. $(3 \times 11) + (42 \times 2.5) - 14 = 33 + 105 - 14 = 124$

E. $\frac{148}{8} + \frac{207}{2} = \frac{148+828}{8} = 122$

2) Answer: C.

I. $|a| < 3 \rightarrow -3 < a < 3$

Multiply all sides by b. Since, $b > 0 \rightarrow -3b < ba < 3b$ (it is true!)

II. Since, $-3 < a < 3, and\ a < 0 \rightarrow -a > a^2 > a$ (plug in $-\frac{1}{3}$, and check!) (It's

false)

III. $-3 < a < 3, multiply\ all\ sides\ by\ 3, then: -9 < 3a < 9$

Subtract 4 from all sides. Then:

$-9 - 4 < 3a - 4 < 9 - 4 \rightarrow -13 < 3a - 4 < 5$ (It is true!)

3) Answer: E.

four years ago, Amy was three times as old as Mike. Mike is 15 years

now. Therefore, 4 years ago Mike was 11 years.

Six years ago, Amy was: $A = 3 \times 11 = 33$

Now Amy is 37 years old: $33 + 4 = 37$

4) Answer: B.

The diagonal of the square is 8. Let x be the side.

Use Pythagorean Theorem: $a^2 + b^2 = c^2$

$x^2 + x^2 = 12^2 \Rightarrow 2x^2 = 12^2 \Rightarrow 2x^2 = 144 \Rightarrow x^2 = 72 \Rightarrow x = \sqrt{72}$

The area of the square is: $\sqrt{72} \times \sqrt{72} = 72$

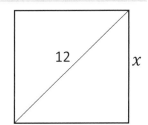

5) Answer: C.

Set of number that are not composite between 11 and 20: A= {11, 13, 17, 19}

Probability $= \dfrac{number\ of\ desired\ outcomes}{number\ of\ total\ outcomes} = \dfrac{4}{10} = \dfrac{2}{5}$

6) Answer: A.

Check each option provided:

A. 13 $\dfrac{3+6+7+10+14}{5} = \dfrac{40}{5} = 8$

B. 6 $\dfrac{3+7+10+13+14}{5} = \dfrac{37}{5} = 9.4$

C. 7 $\dfrac{3+6+10+13+14}{5} = \dfrac{46}{5} = 9.2$

D. 3 $\dfrac{6+7+10+13+14}{5} = \dfrac{50}{5} = 10$

E. 14 $\dfrac{3+6+7+10+13}{5} = \dfrac{39}{5} = 7.8$

7) Answer: C.

The weight of 13.8 meters of this rope is: $13.8 \times 400\ g = 5,520\ g$

1 kg = 1,000 g, therefore, 5,520 g ÷ 1,000 = 5.52 kg

8) Answer: E.

$y = 5ab + 4b^3$

Plug in the values of a and b in the equation: $a = 2$ and $b = 2$

$y = 5\ (2)\ (2) + 4\ (2)^3 = 20 + 4(8) = 20 + 32 = 52$

9) Answer: B.

To find the discount, multiply the number by (100% – rate of discount).

Therefore, for the first discount we get: (D) (100% – 70%) = (D) (0.30) = 0.30 D

For increase of 20 %: (0.30 D) (100% + 20%) = (0.30 D) (1.20) = 0.36 D = 36% of D

10) Answer: B.

100 times the number is 96.4. Let x be the number, then:

$100x = 96.4 \rightarrow x = \frac{96.4}{100} = 0.964$

11) Answer: A.

Let's review the options provided.

A. 5. In 5 years, David will be 75 and Ava will be 15. 75 is 5 times 15.

B. 7. In 7 years, David will be 77 and Ava will be 17. 77 is NOT 5 times 17.

C. 9. In 9 years, David will be 79 and Ava will be 19. 79 is not 5 times 19.

D. 12. In 12 years, David will be 82 and Ava will be 22. 82 is not 5 times 22.

E. 15. In 15 years, David will be 85 and Ava will be 25. 85 is not 5 times 25.

12) Answer: D.

The area of the floor is: 9 cm × 45 cm = 405 cm²

The number is tiles needed = 405 ÷ 15 = 27

13) Answer: B.

$x = 50 + 125 = 175$

14) Answer: D.

By definition, the sine of any acute angle is equal to the cosine of its complement.

Since, angle A and B are complementary angles, therefore:

$\sin B = \cos A$

15) Answer: E.

Solve the system of equations by elimination method.

$2x - 5y = -8$
$-x + 2y = 3$ Multiply the second equation by 2, then add it to the first equation.

$\begin{aligned} 2x - 5y &= -8 \\ 2(-x + 2y &= 3) \end{aligned} \Rightarrow \begin{aligned} 2x - 5y &= -8 \\ -2x + 4y &= 6 \end{aligned} \Rightarrow$ add the equations, $y = 2$

16) Answer: D.

x and z are colinear. y and $6x$ are colinear. Therefore,

$x + z = 2y + 6x, subtract\ x\ from\ both\ sides, then, z = 2y + 5x$

17) Answer: C.

40% of 70 equals to: $0.40 \times 70 = 28$

15% of 600 equals to: $0.15 \times 600 = 90$

40% of 70 is added to 15% of 600: $28 + 90 = 118$

18) Answer: D.

The relationship among all sides of special right triangle

$30°, \ 60°, \ 90°$ is provided in this triangle:

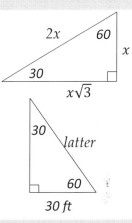

In this triangle, the opposite side of $30°$ angle is half of the

hypotenuse. Draw the shape of this question.

The latter is the hypotenuse.

Therefore, the latter is 60 ft.

19) Answer: A.

The percent of girls playing tennis is: $75\% \times 24\% = 0.75 \times 0.24 = 0.18 = 18\%$

20) Answer: D.

Solve for x. $x^2 + 43 = 130 \Rightarrow x^2 = 57$

Let's review the options.

   A. 5 and 6. $5^2 = 25$ and $6^2 = 36$, 57 is not between these two numbers.

   B. 6 and 7. $6^2 = 36$ and $7^2 = 49$, 57 is not between these two numbers.

   C. 4 and 5. $4^2 = 16$ and $5^2 = 25$, 57 is not between these two numbers.

   D. 7 and 8. $7^2 = 49$ and $8^2 = 64$, 57 is between these two numbers.

   E. 3 and 4. $3^2 = 9$ and $4^2 = 16$, 57 is not between these two numbers.

21) Answer: B.

$(x - 5)^3 = 1 \rightarrow x - 5 = 1 \rightarrow x = 6$

$\rightarrow (x - 5)(x - 2) = (6 - 5)(6 - 2) = (1)(4) = 4$

22) Answer: A.

Add the first 5 numbers. $42 + 44 + 57 + 41 + 52 = 236$

To find the distance traveled in the next 5 hours, multiply the average by number of

hours.

Distance = Average × Rate = 56 × 5 = 280

Add both numbers. 280 + 236 = 516

23) Answer: B.

The question is this: 1.625 is what percent of 1.25

Use percent formula: part = $\frac{\text{percent}}{100}$ × whole

$1.625 = \frac{\text{percent}}{100} \times 1.25 \Rightarrow 1.625 = \frac{\text{percent} \times 1.25}{100} \Rightarrow 162.5 = \text{percent} \times 1.25 \Rightarrow \text{percent} = \frac{162.5}{1.25} = 130$

24) Answer: B.

$\cot\theta = \frac{\text{adjacent}}{\text{opposite}}$

$\cot\theta = \frac{3}{4} \Rightarrow$ we have the following right triangle. Then,

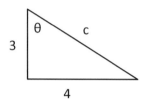

$c = \sqrt{3^2 + 4^2} = \sqrt{9 + 16} = \sqrt{25} = 5$

$\sin\theta = \frac{\text{opposite}}{\text{hypotenuse}} = \frac{4}{5}$

25) Answer: B.

$\frac{2}{5} \cong 0.4 \quad \frac{1}{2} \cong 0.5 \quad \frac{8}{13} \cong 0.61 \quad \frac{5}{7} = 0.71$

26) Answer: C.

Let the number be A. Then:

$y = x\% \times A \rightarrow$ (Solve for A)$\rightarrow y = \frac{x}{100} \times A$

Multiply both sides by $\frac{100}{x}$: $y \times \frac{100}{x} = \frac{x}{100} \times \frac{100}{x} \times A$

$A = \frac{100y}{x}$

27) Answer: C.

$\text{cotangent }\beta = \frac{1}{\text{tangent}\beta} = \frac{1}{\frac{\sqrt{3}}{3}} = \sqrt{3}$

28) Answer: B.

$\frac{3}{8} \times 96 = 36$

29) Answer: B.

One liter=1,000 cm³→ 5 liters=5,000 cm^3

$5,000 = 25 \times 4 \times h \rightarrow h = \frac{5,000}{100} = 50$ cm

30) Answer: C.

Surface Area of a cylinder = $2\pi r \,(r + h)$,

The radius of the cylinder is 3 $(6 \div 2)$ inches and its height is 10 inches. Therefore,

Surface Area of a cylinder = $2\pi\,(3)\,(3 + 10) = 78\,\pi$

31) Answer: C.

7% of the volume of the solution is alcohol. Let x be the volume of the solution.

Then: 7% of $x = 28$ml $\Rightarrow 0.07\,x = 28 \Rightarrow x = 28 \div 0.07 = 400$

32) Answer: B.

$|x - 7| \leq 3 \rightarrow -3 \leq x - 7 \leq 3 \rightarrow -3 + 7 \leq x - 7 + 7 \leq 3 + 7 \rightarrow 4 \leq x \leq 10$

33) Answer: C.

Plug in each pair of number in the equation:

A. $(0, -4)$: $5\,(0) - 2(-4) = 8$ Nope!

B. $(-3, 1)$: $5\,(-3) - 2(1) = -17$ Nope!

C. $(-2, -2)$: $5\,(-2) - 2(-2) = -6$ Bingo!

D. $(1, -2)$: $5\,(1) - 2(-2) = 9$ Nope!

E. $(2, 0)$: $5\,(2) - 2(0) = 5$ Nope!

34) Answer: A.

The area of ΔBED is 16, then: $\frac{8 \times AB}{2} = 16 \rightarrow 8 \times AB = 32 \rightarrow AB = 8$

The area of ΔBDF is 25, then: $\frac{5 \times BC}{2} = 25 \rightarrow 5 \times BC = 50 \rightarrow BC = 10$

The perimeter of the rectangle is $= 2 \times (8 + 10) = 36$

35) Answer: E.

The slop of line A is: $m = \frac{y_2 - y_1}{x_2 - x_1} = \frac{9-8}{3-2} = 1$

Parallel lines have the same slope and only choice E $(y = x)$ has slope of 1.

36) Answer: C.

To solve for $f(5g(p))$, first, find $5g(p)$

$g(x) = \log_5 x \rightarrow g(p) = \log_5 p \rightarrow 5g(p) = 5\log_5 p = \log_5 p^5$

Now, find $f(5g(p))$: $f(x) = 5^x \rightarrow f(\log_5 p^5) = 5^{\log_5 p^5}$

Logarithms and exponentials with the same base cancel each other. This is true

because logarithms and exponentials are inverse operations. Then: $f(\log_5 p^5) = 5^{\log_5 p^5} = p^5$

37) Answer: C.

Write a proportion and solve for x.

$\frac{7}{4} = \frac{x}{68} \Rightarrow 4x = 7 \times 68 \Rightarrow x = 119$ ft

38) Answer: B.

The area of trapezoid is: $\left(\frac{13+22}{2}\right) \times x = 210 \rightarrow 17.5x = 210 \rightarrow x = 12$

$y = \sqrt{9^2 + 12^2} = 15$

Perimeter is: $22 + 12 + 13 + 15 = 62$

39) Answer: B.

$x_1 = \dfrac{7y+\frac{r}{2r+3}}{\frac{z}{6}} = \dfrac{7y+\frac{r}{2r+3}}{\frac{6 \times 12}{z}} = \dfrac{7y+\frac{r}{2r+3}}{6 \times \frac{12}{z}} = \frac{1}{6} \times \dfrac{7y+\frac{r}{2r+3}}{\frac{12}{z}} = \frac{x}{6}$

40) Answer: E.

$0.6x = (0.15) \times 20 \rightarrow x = 5 \rightarrow (x + 6)^2 = (11)^2 = 121$

Answers and Explanations

DAT Mathematics

Practice Tests 6

1) Answer: D.

$830{,}000 = 8.3 \times 10^5$

2) Answer: A.

$(x^5)^{\frac{3}{10}} = x^{5 \times \frac{3}{10}} = x^{\frac{15}{10}} = x^{\frac{3}{2}}$

3) Answer: B.

$\text{average} = \dfrac{\text{sum of terms}}{\text{number of terms}}$

The sum of the weight of all girls is: $25 \times 40 = 1{,}000 \text{ kg}$

The sum of the weight of all boys is: $15 \times 64 = 960 \text{ kg}$

The sum of the weight of all students is: $1{,}000 + 960 = 1{,}960 \text{ kg}$

$\text{average} = \dfrac{1{,}960}{40} = 49$

4) Answer: E.

$y = (-2x^2)^4 = (-2)^4 (x^2)^4 = 16x^8$

5) Answer: B.

The question is this: 399 is what percent of 532?

Use percent formula: $\text{part} = \dfrac{\text{percent}}{100} \times \text{whole}$

$399 = \dfrac{\text{percent}}{100} \times 532 \Rightarrow 399 = \dfrac{\text{percent} \times 625}{100} \Rightarrow 39{,}900 = \text{percent} \times 532 \Rightarrow \text{percent} = \dfrac{39{,}900}{532}$

$= 75$

399 is 75% of 532. Therefore, the discount is: $100\% - 75\% = 25\%$

6) Answer: C.

Plug in the value of x and y. $x = 3$ and $y = -1$

$4(x + y) + (2 - x)^2 = 4(3 + (-1)) + (2 - 3)^2 = 4(3 - 1) + (-1)^2 = 9$

7) Answer: A.

$$\left(\frac{f}{g}\right)(x) = \frac{f(x)}{g(x)} = \frac{3x-7}{x^3-6x}$$

8) Answer: A.

The equation of a line is: $y = mx + b$, where m is the slope and b is the y-intercept.

First find the slope: $m = \frac{y_2 - y_1}{x_2 - x_1} = \frac{8-(-7)}{6-1} = \frac{15}{5} = 3$

Then, we have: $y = 3x + b$

Choose one point and plug in the values of x and y in the equation to solve for b.

Let's choose the point $(1, -7)$

$y = 3x + b \rightarrow -7 = 3(1) + b \rightarrow -7 = 3 + b \rightarrow b = -10$

The equation of the line is: $y = 3x - 10$

9) Answer: B.

Use simple interest formula:

$I = prt$ (I = interest, p = principal, r = rate, t = time)

$I = (12{,}000)(0.015)(4) = 720$

10) Answer: E.

The sum of all angles in a quadrilateral is 360 degrees.

Let x be the smallest angle in the quadrilateral. Then the angles are: $x, 2x, 7x, 8x$

$x + 2x + 7x + 8x = 360 \rightarrow 18x = 360 \rightarrow x = 20$

The angles in the quadrilateral are: $20°, 40°, 140°$, and $160°$

11) Answer: B.

$2sin^2 a + 2cos^2 a = 2(sin^2 a + cos^2 a) = 2(1) = 2$, then:

$x + 2 = 6 \rightarrow x = 4$

12) Answer: C.

Formula for the area of a circle is: $A = \pi r^2$

Using 81 for the area of the circle we have: $81 = \pi r^2$

Let's solve for the radius (r).

$$\frac{81}{\pi} = r^2 \rightarrow r = \sqrt{\frac{81}{\pi}} = \frac{9}{\sqrt{\pi}} = \frac{9}{\sqrt{\pi}} \times \frac{\sqrt{\pi}}{\sqrt{\pi}} = \frac{9\sqrt{\pi}}{\pi} \rightarrow d = 2r = 2 \times \frac{9\sqrt{\pi}}{\pi} \rightarrow d = \frac{18\sqrt{\pi}}{\pi}$$

13) Answer: C.

Length of the rectangle is: $\frac{2}{5} \times 25 = 10$

perimeter of rectangle is: $2 \times (10 + 25) = 75$

14) Answer: E.

The angle x and 50 are complementary angles. Therefore:

$x + 50 = 180 \Rightarrow 180° - 50° = 130°$

15) Answer: B.

Simplify the expression.

$\sqrt{\frac{3x^2}{5} + \frac{x^2}{25}} = \sqrt{\frac{15x^2}{25} + \frac{x^2}{25}} = \sqrt{\frac{16x^2}{25}} = \sqrt{\frac{16}{25}x^2} = \sqrt{\frac{16}{25}} \times \sqrt{x^2} = \frac{4}{5} \times x = \frac{4x}{5}$

16) Answer: A.

Solving Systems of Equations by Elimination

Multiply the first equation by (–4), then add it to the second equation.

$\begin{array}{l} -4(x + 2y = 7) \\ 4x + 5y = 22 \end{array} \Rightarrow \begin{array}{l} -4x - 8y = -28 \\ 4x + 5y = 22 \end{array} \Rightarrow -3y = -6 \Rightarrow y = 2$

Plug in the value of y into one of the equations and solve for x.

$x + 2(2) = 7 \Rightarrow x + 4 = 7 \Rightarrow x = 7 - 4 \Rightarrow x = 3$

17) Answer: A.

The sum of supplement angles is 180. Let x be that angle. Therefore, $x + 9x = 180 \Rightarrow 10x = 180$, divide both sides by 10: $x = 18$

18) Answer: B.

$sin\alpha = \frac{\sqrt{3}}{2} \Rightarrow$ Since $sin\alpha = \frac{opposite}{hypotenuse}$, we have the following right triangle. Then,

$c = \sqrt{2^2 - (\sqrt{3})^2} = \sqrt{4 - 3} = \sqrt{1} = 1$

$cos\alpha = \frac{1}{2}$

19) Answer: A.

The equation of a circle in standard form is:

$(x - h)^2 + (y - k)^2 = r^2$, where r is the radius of the circle.

In this circle the radius is 9. $r^2 = 9 \rightarrow r = 3$

$(x + 3)^2 + (y - 5)^2 = 3^2$

Area of a circle: $A = \pi r^2 = \pi(3)^2 = 9\pi$

20) Answer: E.

Frist factor the function: $f(x) = x^3 + 12x^2 + 32x = x\,(x + 4)(x + 8)$

To find the zeros, $f(x)$ should be zero. $f(x) = x\,(x + 4)(x + 8) = 0$

Therefore, the zeros are: $x = 0$

$(x + 4) = 0 \Rightarrow x = -4$; $(x + 8) = 0 \Rightarrow x = -8$

21) Answer: C.

the population is increased by 20% and 35%. 20% increase changes the population to 120% of original population.

For the second increase, multiply the result by 135%.

$(1.20) \times (1.35) = 1.62 = 162\%$

62 percent of the population is increased after two years.

22) Answer: A.

The relationship among all sides of right triangle $30° - 60° - 90°$ is provided in the following triangle:

Sine of 30° equals to: $\dfrac{opposite}{hypotenuse} = \dfrac{x\sqrt{3}}{2x} = \dfrac{\sqrt{3}}{2}$

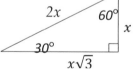

23) Answer: D.

Let x be the length of AB, then: $60 = \dfrac{x \times 8}{2} \rightarrow x = 15$

The length of AC $= \sqrt{15^2 + 20^2} = \sqrt{400} = 25$

The perimeter of $\Delta ABC = 15 + 20 + 25 = 60$

24) Answer: C.

$x_{1,2} = \dfrac{-b \pm \sqrt{b^2 - 4ac}}{2a}$

$ax^2 + bx + c = 0 \Rightarrow 3x^2 + 5x - 8 = 0$, then: a = 3, b = 5 and c = -8

$x = \dfrac{-5 + \sqrt{5^2 - 4 \times 3 \times (-8)}}{2 \times 3} = 1$; $x = \dfrac{-5 - \sqrt{5^2 - 4 \times 3 \times (-8)}}{2 \times 3} = -\dfrac{8}{3}$

25) Answer: A.

Plug in the value of x in the equation and solve for y.

$$5y = \frac{3x^2}{8} + 9 \to 5y = \frac{3(4)^2}{8} + 9 \to 5y = \frac{3(16)}{8} + 9 \to 5y = 6 + 9 = 15$$

$$\to 5y = 15 \to y = 3$$

26) Answer: E.

Use formula of rectangle prism volume.

V = (length) (width) (height) $\Rightarrow$ 5,400 = (15) (12) (height) $\Rightarrow$ height = 5,400 $\div$ 180 = 30

27) Answer: E.

The ratio of boy to girls is 3:5. Therefore, there are 3 boys out of 8 students. To find the answer, first divide the total number of students by 8, then multiply the result by 3.

480 $\div$ 8 = 60 $\Rightarrow$ 60 $\times$ 3 = 180

28) Answer: C.

Plug in the value of each option in the inequality.

A. 1 $(1-2)^2 + 3 > 2(1) + 3 \to 4 > 5$ No!

B. 5 $(5-2)^2 + 3 > 2(5) + 3 \to 12 > 13$ No!

C. 7 $(7-2)^2 + 3 > 2(7) + 3 \to 28 > 17$ Bingo!

D. 2 $(2-2)^2 + 3 > 2(2) + 3 \to 3 > 7$ No!

E. 3 $(3-2)^2 + 3 > 2(3) + 3 \to 4 > 9$ No!

29) Answer: A.

$(x + 3)(x + p) = x^2 + (3 + p)x + 3p \to 3 + p = 4 \to p = 1 \text{ and } r = 3p = 3$

30) Answer: C.

First, find the number.

Let x be the number. Write the equation and solve for x.

200% of a number is 80, then:

$2.0 \times x = 80 \Rightarrow x = 80 \div 2.0 = 40$

70% of 40 is: $0.70 \times 40 = 28$

31) Answer: D.

If the length of the box is 36, then the width of the box is half of it, 18, and the height of the box is 9 (half of the width). The volume of the box is:

V = (length) × (width) × (height) = (36) × (18) × (9) = 5,832

32) Answer: C.

Let x be the smallest number. Then, these are the numbers:

$x, x + 1, x + 2$

average $= \dfrac{\text{sum of terms}}{\text{number of terms}} \Rightarrow 42 = \dfrac{x+(x+1)+(x+2)}{3} \Rightarrow 42 = \dfrac{3x+3}{3} \Rightarrow 126 = 3x + 3 \Rightarrow 123 =$

$3x \Rightarrow x = 41$

33) Answer: D.

Formula for the Surface area of a cylinder is: $SA = 2\pi r^2 + 2\pi rh$

$\rightarrow 88\pi = 2\pi r^2 + 2\pi r(7) \rightarrow r^2 + 7r - 44 = 0$

Factorize and solve for r.

$$(r + 11)(r - 4) = 0 \rightarrow r = 4 \quad or \quad r = -11 \ (unacceptable)$$

34) Answer: B.

The equation of a line in slope intercept form is: $y = mx + b$

Solve for y.

$12x - 4y = 24 \Rightarrow -4y = 24 - 12x \Rightarrow y = (24 - 12x) \div (-4) \Rightarrow$

$y = 3x - 6 \rightarrow$ The slope is 3.

The slope of the line perpendicular to this line is:

$m_1 \times m_2 = -1 \Rightarrow 3 \times m_2 = -1 \Rightarrow m_2 = -\dfrac{1}{3}$

35) Answer: B.

The area of rectangle is: $8 \times 6 = 48 \text{ cm}^2$

The area of circle is: $\pi r^2 = \pi \times (\dfrac{12}{2})^2 = 3 \times 36 = 108 \ cm^2$

Difference of areas is: $108 - 48 = 60$

36) Answer: E.

$$f\big(g(x)\big) = 5 \times (\dfrac{1}{2x})^2 + 8 = \dfrac{5}{4x^2} + 8$$

37) Answer: D.

Use the information provided in the question to draw

the shape. Use Pythagorean Theorem: $a^2 + b^2 = c^2$

$60^2 + 80^2 = c^2 \Rightarrow 3,600 + 64,000 = c^2$

$\Rightarrow 10,000 = c^2 \Rightarrow c = 100$

38) Answer: C.

Let L be the length of the rectangular and W be the with of the rectangular. Then, $L = 7W + 5$

The perimeter of the rectangle is 58 meters. Therefore:

$2L + 2W = 58 \Rightarrow L + W = 29$

Replace the value of L from the first equation into the second equation and solve for

$W: (7W + 5) + W = 29 \to 8W + 5 = 29 \to 8W = 24 \to W = 3$

The width of the rectangle is 4 meters and its length is:

$L = 7W + 5 = 7(3) + 5 = 26$

The area of the rectangle is: length × width = 26 × 3 = 78

39) Answer: A.

$x - 4 \geq 6 \to x \geq 6 + 4 \to x \geq 10$

Or $x - 4 \leq -6 \to x \leq -6 + 4 \to x \leq -2$

Then, solution is: $x \geq 10 \ \cup \ x \leq -2$

40) Answer: E.

Based on triangle similarity theorem:

$\frac{a}{a+b} = \frac{c}{3} \to c = \frac{3a}{a+b} = \frac{3\sqrt{2}}{\sqrt{2}+2\sqrt{2}} = 1$

$\to$ area of shaded region is: $\left(\frac{c+3}{2}\right)(b) = \frac{4}{2} \times 2\sqrt{2} = 4\sqrt{2}$

"End"

Made in the USA
Monee, IL
25 April 2023